The Land God Chose to Love

The Callanish Stones on the Isle of Lewis

THE LAND GOD CHOSE TO LOVE

(An Tir a Roghnaich Dis a Ghradhachadh)

Dr. Brad Allen

Word Association Publishers
205 Fifth Avenue
Tarentum, Pennsylvania 15084

Printed in the United States of America.

ISBN: 1-59571-051-5
Library of Congress Control Number: 200400000

Word Association Publishers
205 Fifth Avenue,
Tarentum, Pennsylvania 15084
www.wordassociation.com

The front and back cover is a landscape view on the Western Shore of The Isle of Lewis.

CONTENTS

1.	Chapter One:	"The Land" (An-Tir)	6
2.	Chapter Two:	"The Revival of 1824-1828" ('Dusgadh 1824-1828)	19
3.	Chapter Three:	"The Revival of 1840-1843" ('Dusgadh 1840-1843)	61
4.	Chapter Four:	"The Revival of 1857-1860" ('Dusgadh 1857-1860)	70
5.	Chapter Five:	"The "Revival of 1900-1903" ('Dusgadh 1900-1903)	79
6.	Chapter Six:	"The Revival of 1923-1926" ('Dusgadh 1923-1926)	86
7.	Chapter Seven:	"The Revival of 1934-1939" ('Dusgadh 1934-1939)	89
8.	Chapter Eight:	"The Revival of 1949-1953" ('Dusgadh 1949-1953)	131
9.	Chapter Nine:	"The Revival of 1960-1965" ('Dusgadh 1960-1965)	157
10.	Chapter Ten:	"The Revival of 1969-1973" ('Dusgadh 1969-1973)	164
11.	Chapter Eleven:	"The Revival of 1984-1986" ('Dusgadh1984-1986)	179
12.	Chapter Twelve:	"The Isle of Lewis Today" (Eilean Leodhas An-Diugh)	197

PREFACE

My fascination with the Isle of Lewis had its beginning in 1988 when I was given a set of five audio cassette tapes containing the preaching of Duncan Campbell, the Scottish Highlander preacher. He was the principal preacher of the Lewis Revival of 1949-53. After many years of research, I completed a book on this great revival, which was released in May, 2002 under the title, *Catch the Wind*. As I did research for that book, I became aware that the Isle of Lewis was no stranger to revival. In fact, many great revivals have come to this island, beginning in 1824..

The springboard which launched this book happened on the night of August 20, 2003. What I am about to relate may seem strange to some, but I will tell it exactly as it happened.

I was in the state of Colorado preaching for the summer. During my sleep on that August night, I had a dream. Whether it was a dream, or a vision, I do not know. But God came to me in a very vivid way and told me to write a book on the history of revival on the Isle of Lewis. In this dream, the title of the book came to me, the chapters were told to me. I was also instructed to give the title of the book, and the chapter titles in both English and Gaelic, the native language of the Western Highlands of Scotland and the Hebrides Islands. I do not know or understand why, but I have simply done what I was told to do.

No study I have ever done has thrilled my heart as the study of revival on the Isle of Lewis. It is a story of God in action, a history of a people who came from hard circumstances to find rest in a Loving God. It is a story of a land that God chose to love.

I will always be indebted to Dr. Roy Fish, Professor at Southwestern Baptist Theological Seminary who first got me interested in the preaching of Duncan Campbell. His life, his passion for revival has impacted my life in a most unusual way. For that, I want to thank him.

I also want to thank Dr. Ron Phillips, Pastor of the Central Baptist Church, Hixon, Tennessee, for making me aware of the workings of the Blessed Holy Spirit in one's life. As you read of revival on the Isle of Lewis, you realize that the Holy Spirit came down and did a work that cannot be explained outside of HIM.

My appreciation is also extended to Dr. R. T. Kendall, former Pastor of the Westminster Chapel, London, England, for taking me down the road to the meaning of total forgiveness, and the spiritual power that can come from total forgiveness.

It is also needful that I thank my wife, Nancy, who has traveled every step of the way in my journey with the Lord. Through the years of the pastorate, she was always there. During these past five years of preaching Spiritual Awakening Conferences across America, Nancy has been faithful in every way. She has prayed for me, encouraged me, and traveled with me. This book would not be possible without her.

I will also be eternally grateful to the Blessed Lord for speaking to me in the mountains of Colorado. I thank HIM for giving me a passion to see revival in our day.

I also want to extend my gratitude to David Fowler, Senior Librarian for Adult Services at the Stornoway Library, and Janet Nicolson, who works for the Stornoway Gazette newspaper. Both of these dear people gave me assistance that was invaluable.

Chapter one

"THE LAND"
(AN TIR)

The Isle of Lewis is one of the Hebrides Islands. The Hebrides consist of two groups of islands off the northwest coast of Scotland. The group of islands closest to the mainland of Scotland is called the Inner Hebrides, while the group located farther west is called the Outer Hebrides. Lewis is the northern most island of the Outer Hebrides.

The official name of the Isle of Lewis is "Lewis on Harris." The northern part of the island is called Lewis, while the southern part is called Harris. It is the largest island of the entire group of 500 of the Hebrides. The northern part of the island is low and wet. Peat bogs cover most of its surface. The southern part of the island has mountains, shining sea lochs and hidden valleys with earth and life.

The Land of Lewis is harsh and rugged. The climate is wet, with fierce winds blowing in from the Atlantic Ocean almost constantly. As one drives across Lewis, you notice immediately the absence of trees. Not a tree in sight!

The people of Lewis are friendly, outgoing, gregarious people. On my trip to Lewis in October, 2001, I discovered the most kind, gracious people I have ever met.

Through the centuries, the people of Lewis have known their share of problems; poverty, hunger, starvation, and mass migration of its people to other lands. But, in the midst of all of their problems, the people of Lewis have an inward peace about them. They have the peace of a people of a classless society. They live in a land, "where no man commands another. They can risk friendliness, and they do." (1)

Across the centuries, the native language of Lewis has been the Gaelic. Over the years, I have studied Latin, Greek and Hebrew, but, this is most difficult language I have ever encountered. The people of the Hebrides have had a fierce struggle over the centuries in guarding and protecting their language. The government of Scotland tried to stamp it out. The invasion of the English language threatened to make the Gaelic extinct.

In the last half of the 19th Century and the first half of the 20th Century, the Gaelic language was dying a slow death. From 1891 to 1951, the number of Gaelic speakers dropped from 250,000 to 95,000. (2) The radical drop in Gaelic speakers was due to two things; the influence of the English language, and the way Lowland Scotland looked upon the Gaelic language. Lowland Scotland believed those who spoke Gaelic were the backward, uneducated. English was the language of the elite, Gaelic was the language of the unlearned. As the Gaelic language dropped in popularity, it became the language spoken in the rural areas and the small villages of the Highlands and the Western Islands.

But, those who spoke the Gaelic believed their language was very precious. They clung to it with a hard grip. One Lewis Crofter (farmer) said, "We belong to this place. I'm a Gaelic-speaking man. We all had the Gaelic once, but now we're growing few, and our tongue is being lost, and the language holds the tales, and the tales hold the knowledge of the old ways and the old days, of holy and unholy things. (3)

But, today there is a resurgence of Gaelic. It is being taught in schools, and in special Gaelic classes. The people of Lewis love to speak the Gaelic, and to hear it spoken. They especially love to hear the Word of God preached in the Gaelic.

It was to the Isle of Lewis that God cast His eye a long time ago. The first great revival came to this island in 1828, and other revivals have followed through the years. Why? I wish I had the answer to that.

The Isle of Lewis is a land God chose to love. Perhaps the

day will come, in the corridors of eternity, that we will understand why God put His hand on this land, but, while living on this earth, we will continually be asking the question, "Does God look with favor on a certain location?" Does God cast an eye on a certain community or city and say, "I am going to put my love in that place!" I believe in the Sovereignty of God, however, we can never negate human responsibility. When God really comes on a place in real revival it may be that the people of that area are more prepared, more open, more willing to receive the blessing of the Lord. It is evident to me that God looks out from His throne in heaven and looks with favor on certain places.

Charles Finney, the famous American evangelist said in his "Lectures on Systematic Theology",

> "We have seen, that none come to the Christ, except they are drawn of the Father, and that the Father draws to Christ, those and those only whom He has given to Christ, and also, that it is the Father's design that of those whom He has given to Christ, He should lose none, but that he should raise them up at the last day. This is the only hope that any will be saved. Strike out this foundation, and what will the righteous do? Strike out from the Bible the doctrine of God's covenanted faithfulness to Christ, the truth that the Father has given him a certain number whose salvation He foresees that he could and should secure, and I despair of myself and of everybody else. Where is any ground of hope? I know not where!"

God is sovereign over His entire universe. He does not "jump through a hoop" every time we follow a prescribed set of rules, or after we have prayed a certain number of hours.

BUT, we must never use the sovereignty of God as an excuse for our lack of action. It is horrible for us to blame God for our cold hearts. Duncan Campbell used to say, "I believe in the sovereignty of God, but I do not believe in any sovereignty of God that nullifies human responsibility." (4)

Whatever you believe about the Sovereignty of God and human responsibility, by the time you reach the end of this book, I believe you will agree that the Isle of Lewis is a land God chose to love.

LONGING FOR LIGHT

The Isle of Lewis is a strange, wonderful land. In the town of Stornoway, the largest town on the island, there are trees that have been planted across the years. But, when you leave Stornoway, and drive across the island, there is not a tree in sight. The landscape of Lewis is one of continuous peat bogs and heather. A drive across the island is both, lonely and thrilling, monotonous and captivating, ugly and beautiful. One has difficulty in explaining this, but all of these emotions are present at the same time. You watch the heather blowing in the fierce winds that come straight off the Atlantic Ocean, you observe the sheep grazing aimlessly beside the highway, and suddenly you are caught with the thought that this is a land God chose to love.

In the 18th and 19th Centuries, the people of Lewis were in the proper position to be longing for a light from God. Life on the Isle of Lewis was bleak and hard. When the 18th Century dawned, the people of Lewis were living in abject darkness. This darkness encompassed their social, political, and religious life.

Socially, life of the Isle of Lewis was one of misery, hard labor, and no hope. They lived in "blackhouses." These houses had rock walls, and thatched-roofs, constructed to withstand the cold and fierce winds. They had long, rounded ends, having the livestock under the same roof with the people. There was a partition between the livestock and the living quarters. The "Blackhouse" had no chimney and no floors. The only fire with which to heat or to cook was a pile of peat in the middle of the floor. The smoke from the fire had to find its way out of the house through the thatched roof. The islanders of Lewis were "crofters" (farmers), living and working a small piece of ground that would never belong to them. All of the land was owned by absentee landlords, who lived on the mainland of Scotland or in England.

The people of Lewis made their living by farming and fishing. The farming was meager. Very little of the land is arable. The little bit of land that could be farmed was laid off in small ridged plots called "feannagan taomaidh", lazy-beds. There were five classes of farm tenants on Lewis:

1. Tacksmen, who held their land direct from the proprietor for a period of nineteen years.
2. Small tenants, who held their lands direct from the proprietor on a verbal lease of one year.
3. Sub-tenants, who held their land from the tacksmen. This was the category that most people were in.
4. The cottars or farm servants
5. The "sgalag", menial. (5)

Fishing was very popular in Lewis, not out of sport, but out of necessity. Fishing was done on the open sea and in the lochs and streams of Lewis. There is an old proverb of the Hebrides Islands, "Dh'iarr am muir a thadhal" "The sea wants to be visited." Across the centuries the people of Lewis did visit the sea to supplement their income from the land. Consequently, fishing has become an art on Lewis. When

Morris West wrote about fishing on the Isle of Lewis, he said about fishermen,

"They are all fanatics.....They worship always in solitary places: by dark pools and mountain streams and hidden arms of the sea. They are jealous of these private shrines and apt to be hostile to intruders. They measure salvation by the pound, and the merit of a man by his skill with a fighting fish. You will recognize them by their ruddy, patient faces and their faraway eyes and the colored flies stuck on their hats. .....They would submit to martyrdom rather than use a gill net, and some of them mourn the old days when a poacher could be legally killed with a spring gun or exiled to the Colonies for taking a trout from another man's water."(6)

Fergus William McCue, the fisherman in West's novel, in telling about the art of fishing said,

"It's a patient art, laddie, as you've now seen. It's like the painting of a picture or the carving of an angel out of a chunk of marble. It's the art of the hands, but it's also of the mind because you must know what a fish will be doing with himself while you're bending your wits to catch him. And even when you've hooked him, you have to know how far he'll run and when you can begin reeling him in." (7)

For the people of Lewis, fishing, farming a small bit of ground, and raising a few head of livestock was their total existence.

Politically, the people of Lewis were totally without influence. They had no vote, no voice, no ties to any of the decision-makers of Scotland. They lived virtually as slaves on the island.

Religiously, the islanders lived in sheer darkness. Through the centuries there had been imbedded in the people of Lewis a deep belief in witches, ghosts and other superstitions. When the 18th Century came, the Isle of Lewis was little more than pagan in their beliefs. The Callanish Stones of Lewis stand as silent sentinels to the paganism of the past. Located southwest of the town of Stornoway, the Callanish Stones are a group of forty-two stones set in the form of a cross with a circle at its juncture. It is the form of a Celtic cross. Scholars believe these stones may be a prehistoric calendar, or they may mark the site of a temple where the early Celts worshiped Bel, the sun god. These stones were set 3,000 to 4,000 years ago, and stand as an example of the dark, pagan atmosphere which shrouded the Isle of Lewis for centuries.

There were several things that set the stage for the coming of the gospel of Jesus Christ to the Isle of Lewis. Many things set up in the hearts of the people a longing for light.

THE EDUCATION ACT OF 1616- For many years the British government did everything possible to repress the Gaelic language. The people of the Western Highlands of Scotland, and the Hebrides Islands, who spoke the Gaelic language, were looked upon by the Scottish lowlanders and the English as an inferior race of people. The object of the Education Act of 1616 was, "that the Irishe (Gaelic) language, which is one of the chief and principal causes of the barbarite and incivilite among the inhabitents of the Isles and Heylandis, may be abolished and removit." (8)

This Education Act of 1616 was ratified in 1631 and again in 1646. It stated that a network of schools would be established in every parish to instruct the young in godliness and knowledge and to teach them to read and write in the English language at the expense of Gaelic. The outcome was several generations of people who did not learn to read or to write in any language. For instance, in the early 1800's, a sample of three Highland and four Island parishes, of a population of 22,501, 19,376 were unable to read or write in either English or Gaelic. (9)

The people of the Isle of Lewis lived in harsh, horrible conditions, unable to read or write. If they had been able to read and write, there were no books and no Bible in the Gaelic language, so they sat in spiritual darkness.

THE PATRONAGE ACT OF 1712- Patronage was the system whereby the head of the family who had financed the building of a church had the right to choose its minister. Through the years the right of appointment of the church ministers had gone to the Presbyteries, but the Patronage Act of 1712 restored the right of the local landowners to choose the minister of his church. This practice only deepened the spiritual darkness of the people. Wealthy landowners appointed relatives and friends as church ministers who did not know God, or else were of such a modernist bent that the gospel of Jesus Christ never got to the people. Many of the church ministers appointed under this patronage system were drunks, little caring about the spiritual lives of the people.

THE HIGHLAND CLEARANCES OF 1782- For many years, the demand for beef was high because of the fighting of foreign wars. Once the wars were over, the demand for beef ceased and the wealthy noblemen faced bankruptcy. As the demand for beef declined, the demand for sheep and wool rose to an all-time high. The wealthy landlords saw an opportunity to replace their herds of cattle with flocks of sheep. The raising of sheep became a highly profitable enterprise. While cattle had to be cared for, looked after, sheep could be left to wander the hills and glens at will, with only a shepherd to see after them. The landowners soon found out that one shepherd would take up as much land as 12 to 18 families who farmed and raised cattle. In four of the Highland areas, where there had been 355,000 sheep, that number rose to two million.

When the Highland Clearance Act was formalized, large numbers of people in the Highlands and the Hebrides Islands were moved off the land they farmed to make room for more sheep. This clearance was devastating to the people. In the 1800's, the verified number of people who were moved off the Isle of Lewis because of the Highland Clearances was 6,700.(10) Remembering that the large number of those who were moved cannot be verified because there were no records kept. Many of those who were "cleared out" of Lewis moved to Australia, Canada, Nova Scotia, and America. A ship would pull into a loch at night, and the next morning an entire village would be found deserted of people. One cannot fathom the emotions as people were jerked from the only home they had ever known. One eyewitness to these partings in the islands said,

> "I could see a long and motley procession winding along the road that led north from Suisnish. It halted at the point of the road opposite Kilbride. And there the lamentation became loud and long. As I drew near I could see that the minister with his wife and daughters had come out to meet the people and bid them farewell. It was a miscellaneous gathering of at least three generations of crofters. There were old men and women too feeble to walk placed on carts. Everyone was in tears; each wished to clasp the hand of the minister that had so often befriended them. When they set forth again, a cry of grief went up to heaven, the long plaintive wail like a funeral coronach was resumed, and after the last of the emigrants had disappeared behind, the sound

seemed to re-echo through the whole valley of Strath in one prolonged note of desolation. The people were on their way to be shipped to Canada." (11)

The Highland Clearances devastated and depleted the Isle of Lewis. Neighbors were torn from neighbors. Family members were jerked away from other family members. Thousands of islanders were cast aboard ships to sail to foreign lands about which they knew nothing. The sons and daughters of Lewis were scattered across the world. An anonymous man from the Isle of Skye wrote in far-off Canada:

From the lone shieling of the misty island
Mountains divide us, and the waste of seas;
Yet still the blood is strong, the heart is Highland,
And we in dreams behold the Hebrides.(12)

THE GREAT DISRUPTION OF 1843- Church life in Scotland has had a turbulent past. The Reformed Church in Scotland came into being in 1560. It became known as the Established Church of Scotland. The word, established, means that by an act of parliament, it was established as the National Church and would be connected with the state, and would enjoy a privileged position. This privileged position soon began to bear a cost as the state began to interfere in the life of the church. In the 17th Century, an attempt was made by the state to introduce bishops. This led to the persecution of the "Covenanters", those who covenanted together to maintain the freedom of the church.

This eventually led to a split in the church which brought about the Secession Church in 1733. Then, in 1761, the formation of the Relief Church was begun by Thomas Gillespie.

There was a third split in 1843 which has become known

as the Great Disruption. This disruption was led by Thomas Chalmers and led to the formation of the Free Church of Scotland. While the Seceder and Relief movements saw only a scattered few join their ranks, the Great Disruption of 1843 saw over 400 ministers resign from the Church of Scotland. After the Great Disruption of 1843, the Free Church became the main denomination on the Isle of Lewis. All but two of the church ministers on Lewis left the Church of Scotland. Most of the church members followed. Those who left the established church were left with no church building, no pulpit, no meeting place but the open vales and glens of an area.

There then followed a series of church unions. In 1847 the Secession church and the Relief Church merged to become the United Presbyterian Church. In 1900 the Free Church merged with the United Presbyterian Church to become the United Free Church. A minority did not go into that merger and continue today as the Free Church of Scotland. In 1929 the United Free Church merged with the Established Church of Scotland. A minority did not enter this merger and continue today as the United Free Church.

It was into this cauldron of events that the people of the Isle of Lewis found themselves thrown; no education, illiterate, churches led by ministers who could not, or would not preach the gospel of Christ, the Highland Clearances which ripped apart the society of the island, and church splits which further divided the people. It was this society of people on the Isle of Lewis that kept on longing for some light. It was to these people that the light did come in great, wonderful, impossible spiritual awakening. O, to think! God came down in all of His glory on the Isle of Lewis. It was this little island, Lewis, that God chose to love.

THEN, in 1824 revival came! As you read through these great movements of God on this island, you will find some common threads that brought about revival. We should take seriously some lessons; that where the Son is God is believed and obeyed, where His gospel is truly and sincerely preached, where His people are penitent and humble, where His people are prayerful and absolutely open to the Living God, Almighty God will fulfill His promise:

> "But on this one will I look; on him who is poor and of a contrite spirit, and who trembles at My word.....For as soon as Zion was in labor, she gave birth to her children.....As a mother comforts her child, so I will comfort you; and you will be comforted over Jerusalem....When you see this, your heart will rejoice and you will flourish as grass." (Isaiah 66:2,8,13,14) (13)

Why this island? Why did God come in all His glory to the land of Lewis? I will not even pretend to answer that question fully in this book. To do that, one would have to know the mind of God. However, I do believe we can understand some of the workings of God in the land of Lewis. Through the years, the Isle of Lewis was separated from the rest of the world in many different ways. The island was a journey of several hours by boat from the mainland of Scotland. The island stood alone, isolated, developing its own culture, its own beliefs, its own life.

Since the Isle of Lewis was that small, isolated land, one cannot help but think of the Word of God. The Apostle Paul wrote, "But God has chosen the foolish things of the world to put to shame the wise; and God has chosen the weak things of the world to put to shame the things which are mighty; and the base things of the world and the things which are despised God has chosen , and the things which are not, to bring to nothing the things that are, that no flesh should glory in His presence" (I Cor. 1:27-29).

God did not pick Rome, Paris, New York City, nor any of the great cities of the world to show His glory. He put to shame the wise of the world, and picked out Lewis, little Lewis, to come down and reveal Himself to the world.

Chapter two

"THE REVIVAL OF 1824-1828"

('DUSGADH 1824-1828)

A man from the Isle of Lewis had a dream. In the dream he saw a man arriving on the shore of Lewis with the sun resting on his shoulder. Afterwards this Lewis man was filled with joy when he saw the same man from the dream disembarking from a boat at Stornoway. The man getting off the boat was Mr. Alexander Macleod, whom God was to use in mighty power to bring revival to Lewis. Macleod had been appointed as the church minister at Uig, a village on the southwest corner of the Isle of Lewis. Since it was the day of Patronage, Alexander Macleod had been appointed to this position by Mrs. Stewart Mackenzie, whose husband was the landowner of Lewis at that time. Mrs. Mackenzie was in favor of evangelical ministers, and had appointed Macleod to the church in Uig in hopes of seeing spiritual awakening come to the area. Macleod was appointed in 1823. He visited Lewis in January, 1824 and sent a report to Mrs. Mackenzie, "I have heart-felt satisfaction of giving you good tidings of great joy. Through the whole island there is a great thirst for religious instruction and information." (1)

Macleod was a farmer's son. He was born in 1786 a few miles south of Cape Wrath in Assynt in the northern part of the mainland of Scotland. When Macleod was growing up, the spiritual life of his area was very, very low. The minister in his parish church was more given to whiskey than to the Bible. When he was fourteen years of age, the Holy Spirit awakened him to the need of salvation. He traveled, near and far, to hear preachers. He went to Ferintosh and heard great preachers whom Charles Calder had gathered, and it was there Alexander Macleod found peace in Jesus Christ. He was licensed to preach in Tongue on November 26, 1818, and ordained in the Gaelic Church in Dundee on December 16, 1819. From Dundee Macleod moved to the Gaelic Church in

Cromarty on the eastern side of the mainland of Scotland. From Cromarty, he came to the Isle of Lewis.

He assumed the pastorate of the Uig Church, a congregation of over 800 people. Most of them were pagans. His first Sunday service was marked by the lively buying and selling of the people in front of the church. One man was serving whisky from a jar, another was busy selling tobacco. This Sabbath desecration filled Macleod with anger. He attacked these practices at once. He said, "If you slacken your reins for a mile, the devil will drive the rest of the journey." (2)

The condition of Lewis in the early 1800's was total, complete spiritual darkness. Not one ray of spiritual sunlight was shining. But, gospel light is on its way. There was a deep thirst in the hearts of the people to know God, but they had no way to find Him. As early as 1822, there were signs of spiritual awakening, but it mostly exhibited itself in a great upheaval and unrest among the people. Things began to happen that people could not explain. On the Isle of Lewis, the year of 1822 became known as "Bliadhna an fhaomaidh", "the year of the swoonings." In the presence of God, people began to swoon, or fall under His power.

The revival of 1824-28 did not come about overnight. It was the culmination of several years of unique events that brought about the coming of the glory of God on the Isle of Lewis. For almost 200 years, there had been a concentrated effort on the part of the government to completely wipe out the Gaelic language. By 1800, very few of the common people of the Highlands and the Islands could read or write. There was no translation of the New Testament into the Scottish Gaelic until 1767, and the entire Bible was not published in Gaelic until 1801. Through all of those years, the only way the people could have the Word of God read to them in their own language was by immediate oral translation. There were some of the evangelical ministers in the Highlands who had trained themselves to read directly from English and speak it in the Gaelic. However, the vast majority of the people were totally illiterate.

In 1709, the "Society for Propagating Christian Knowledge" was formed, and in 1725 the "Royal Bounty" was founded. These two societies began to establish schools and mission stations to teach the people to read and write. The end purpose of both of these societies was to bring the gospel of Jesus Christ to the people.

By 1811, the "Society for Propagating Christian Knowledge" had 290 schools in the Highlands and the Islands, teaching sixteen thousand students. But, these students were only taught in English because there was no Gaelic material that was available to the common people. It was not until 1828 that the complete Gaelic Bible was available at a price the common people could afford. (3)

On January 16, 1811, the Gaelic School Society held its first meeting in Edinburgh. They decided at that meeting the dire necessity of teaching the people of the Highlands and the Islands to read and write in their own language. They resolved at that meeting, "by the erection of circulating schools for the express purpose of instructing them in the Gaelic language....to teach the inhabitants to read the Holy Scriptures." One of the rules of the Gaelic School Society was that the teachers who were to be employed by the Society would neither be preachers nor public exhorters of any denomination. The Society did not want their teaching to infringe on the position of Church Ministers.

The Gaelic School Society began sending out "Catechists", those who would go to a certain area and teach the people to read and write. They would use the Psalms and the Shorter Catechism as the beginning point. There were three types of schools where the Catechists would teach; the parish school, the schools supported by the Society for the Propagation of Christian Knowledge, and the schools supported by the Gaelic School Society.

Many of the Highland and Island Catechists, serving in these different types of schools, were men of outstanding character. They were wonderful, godly men who saw the blessing of God on their work in both the conversion of the lost and the building up of believers. Many of these Catechists went on to become great preachers.

The response to the schools was overwhelming. It was not unusual to see a grandchild and a grandmother sitting in the same classroom, learning to read and write. In Glencalvie, in the parish of Kincardine, Ross-shire in 1815, the Catechist had a student who had seen three centuries. His name was Iverach. He had been a young soldier at the time of the Jacobite uprising of 1715. He had such a desire to learn to read and write that, at the age of 117, he joined the Gaelic class and became an enthusiastic, and not unsuccessful student. (4)

THE COMING OF REVIVAL

When Alexander Macleod stepped ashore at the town of Stornoway in 1824, he little expected the things that were in store in the next few years. When Macleod landed in Stornoway, a man named Murdo Macdonald met him at the landing and asked, "Who constituted you to be my catechiser?" Macleod replied, "The Spirit of God did! I came from Stoer in Assynt. There I was born and brought up. I have been minister in Dundee, and at Cromarty, and am going to Uig."

Macdonald asked, "What are you to do in Uig?" Macleod said, "To give the people the simple gospel in all of its glory and wonder." Macdonald said, "It's sorely needed in Uig. There's not a soul in that parish knows anything about it except one herd laddie, and they call him stark mad." (5)

It is interesting to note that the young herd laddie Murdo Macdonald was referring to was a young lad named Malcolm Macritchie, who later became the Pastor at Knock. In 1818, there were only two Bibles in the parish of Uig, one in the church, and the other in the manse (parsonage). That year, Malcolm Macritchie was loaned a New Testament in Gaelic by a friend in another part of the island. He also acquired a copy of Richard Baxter's, *Call to the Unconverted*, and Joseph Alleine's, *Alarm to the Unconverted*. Through the reading of these three volumes, Macritchie came under conviction. He had no one to guide him to salvation. In 1820, he heard that an entire Gaelic Bible was for sale in Stornoway. He walked the thirty miles to purchase one. When he arrived in Stornoway, he found that the price was five shillings, more than he had. A few days after he returned home, he found a cask of palm oil that had washed up on shore from a ship wreckage. He reported it to the Custom-house in Stornoway and received five shillings for it. He immediately set off for Stornoway and purchased the Gaelic Bible. Sometime during the year of 1820, Malcolm Macritchie not only obtained the treasure of a Gaelic Bible, but also the treasure of eternal life in Jesus Christ.

When word began to spread through the parish of Uig that Malcolm Macritchie had a Bible, the neighbors began to gather to hear him read it. The Church Minister, Mr. Munro, was very unhappy about it, and threatened to remove Malcolm's father from his land. Malcolm's father replied, "You can take the land from me, but you cannot take grace from Malcolm." (6)

By 1823, Malcolm Macritchie was teaching the Bible in different places. Children, parents and grandparents would attend his teaching. A few years later, Malcolm Macritchie became a Church Minister and spent the rest of his life laboring in three different congregations.

Alexander Macleod assumed the pastorate of the Uig Church in 1824. As stated previously, Macleod found a church with 800 members, but most of them pagans. On the Sabbath Day, the church members would gather in front of the church, selling whiskey and tobacco. When Macleod held his first prayer meeting in the church, he was shocked to hear one of the Elders pray, "O Lord, you know we have come a long way to this meeting. We have put ourselves to a good deal of trouble, and we hope that you will reward us for it by casting some wreck on the shore on our way home." The people of Uig made some income by gathering supplies from ship wrecks along the ocean shore. At the same prayer meeting, another man prayed, "Is latha dubh dhuinne an latha bhasaich Criosd." He was speaking of the death of Christ on the cross as a great calamity. Macleod said, "Sit down, man, sit down! You have said enough." (7)

Macleod began a serious, deep prayer life. In light of the spiritual ignorance of his people, he went to his knees. Macleod became a prince in prayer. His sermons had always been pleasant and easy, but suddenly his preaching became like arrows of fire, shooting into the hearts of the people. Within a few months, the listeners sat in a holy hush, tears streaming down their faces.

In the Highlands and the Islands, Communion Season (The Lord's Supper) is a huge event in the life of a church.

Communion there is nothing like communion in churches in America. There are usually two Communion Seasons in the church each year. Communion Season begins on Wednesday and concludes on Monday. A Church will meet day and night. When it is Communion Season, work stops, schools close, shops shut their doors. Everyone concentrates on God.

Wednesday is the Pre-Communion Prayer Service. Thursday is Fast Day. People give themselves to waiting upon God. Friday is the men's meeting. The men are asked to give their testimonies. On Saturday, the people appear before the ministers. They must give a testimony of having been saved by sovereign grace and must live accordingly. Those who pass this examination are given a token to sit at the Lord's Table. Then comes Sunday! There are usually five sermons on Sunday; the Action Sermon, the Sensing of the Table Sermon, making it clear who ought to be at the Lord's Table, and who ought not be at the Lord's Table, a sermon before the sacraments are administered, a sermon following the sacraments, and, last, a sermon of guidance, comfort and strength to God's people.

When Alexander Macleod became Pastor of the Uig Church in 1824, there were between 800 and 900 communicants. A communicant was one who came forward and took the Lord's Supper during the Communion Season. However, Macleod soon noticed that godliness was a stranger to the people. Family worship was unknown. Superstition abounded. Macleod began to question the people, and found they were totally ignorant of the great truths of the Bible. When he preached, the people were at a loss as to what he was saying. As Macleod moved among the people, he found only a few who knew the names of Adam and Eve. Of Noah, the patriarchs and the prophets, they knew nothing. When

Macleod asked how many sacraments Christ appointed, most of the people answered, "Seven." When Macleod asked the people on what they based their salvation, almost all of the people said that good conduct and doing the best they could was the grounds of their salvation. Swearing, lying, stealing, uncleanness, and drunkenness were rampant.

Because of the spiritual ignorance of the people, Macleod decided not to set a Communion Season during his first year at Uig. When his second year, 1826, came, Macleod again decided not to administer the Lord's Supper at the church. Finally, on June 24, 1827, Macleod had a Lord's Supper service at the church. This Communion Season had been preceded by the instituting of prayer meetings, biblical preaching, and the appointment of teachers who taught in the schools the Word of God. This Communion Season was vastly different from the past. Before, everyone would come to the Lord's Table. But, at the Communion of 1827, with a crowd of between 800-1000 people, when the call to the Lord's Table was given, only six people came forward. Macleod said, "When the elements were presented, there appeared as a shower of revival from the presence of the Lord through the whole congregation, and in serving the first and second tables, the heavenly dew of gracious influences was evidently falling down on the people.......While these things were carried on, the ungodly were in tears, and iniquity for a time dwindled into nothing. (8)

The next year, June 25, 1828, the Rev. John Macdonald of Ferintosh preached the sermon. It made a deep impression on the people, and the gentle breezes of revival began to spread through the parish of Uig. John Macdonald of Ferintosh was the Highland preacher who became known as the "Apostle of the North." Macdonald of Ferintosh had been on his way to the Island of St. Kilda, but bad weather prevented him from landing at St. Kilda. He landed at Harris and made his way across the Isle of Lewis to Uig. He and his son arrived in Uig on June 22, 1827 and Macdonald preached on Saturday, Sunday and Monday. The stated number present on Sunday was 7,000..

People began to come to Uig from all parts of the island. A spiritual awakening was evidently in progress. When the Communion Season came in 1828, the estimate of the crowd was from 9,000 to 11,000 people who gathered

The center of attention for all the Isle of Lewis became the preaching of Alexander Macleod. A great thirst for the gospel of Christ rose on the island. People made their way to Uig from Ness, Back, Knock, distances up to forty miles for the preaching services. Macleod said in his diary, "O, how much have I to praise the Lord for His goodness to my people....They now come to me from every corner crying, What shall we do to be saved?'.....Glory be to God for this wonderful change! May I never forget His benefits! Blessed be God for His unspeakable gift!" (9)

The revival in Uig seemed to grow in its intensity. By 1833 large numbers of people from Harris and the Island of Uist were attending Communion Season in Uig. A naval captain, whose ship was lying off the coast at Uig, said, "At all hours, from 8:00 P.M. to 1:00 A.M., I have heard people at prayer as I passed by. They are an extraordinary people here; one cannot but be struck with their honesty, kindness, and sobriety. I think I have never seen a drunk person out of the town. One hears of religion elsewhere, but one sees it here in everything." (10)

Alexander Macleod stayed at the Uig Church until 1844. When the Great Disruption occurred in the Church of

Scotland in 1843, and the Free Church was formed, Macleod joined the Free Church movement. In 1844, Macleod moved to a church in Lochalsh, stayed for three years, then to a church in Rogart where he remained for twenty-three years. He died in 1869. Although he made a deep, lasting impression on his people in Rogart, he never again saw great revival as he did in Uig.

Of the revival at Uig, Professor George Smeaton said that it was the purest revival that he knew of in the history of the Church in Scotland. (11)

MEN AND WOMEN OF THE UIG REVIVAL

To have a fuller understanding of the Uig Revival of 1824-28, one must take a look at the men and women who made a difference in the Kingdom of God during this time. Their stories are varied and deeply interesting. Their lives hold stories of people who were touched by the Living God, and, for them, life was never the same again.

MALCOLM MACRITCHIE- When Alexander Macleod landed at the dock in Stornoway in 1824 to take charge of the Uig Church, a man met him at the dock and told him there was not a soul in Uig who knew anything about the gospel of Christ except one young herd laddie, and they think he is stark mad. That young herd laddie was Malcolm Macritchie. Macritchie had bought a copy of the Gaelic Bible in 1821, and the contents of that Book became a treasure to his soul. When he was under conviction of sin, Macritchie went to the manse to talk to his Minister, Mr. Munro, who was not an evangelical preacher. All the doors of the manse were locked and the maids were peeping through the windows. They were terrified, for the Minister, Mr. Munro, had told them Malcolm was insane.

Macritchie went on to teach the Bible at Aline and Lochs. He traveled to the Isle of Skye to sit under the teaching of Donald Munro, the blind catechist of Snizort, Skye. Macritchie said, late in his life, "I have heard several of the Disruption worthies delivering sermons on humility, but never heard any who would come up to Donald Munro." (12) He became a Minister, and served three congregations of believers.

ANGUS MACLEOD-Of all the works of God in the Uig Revival, none is more thrilling and mysterious than that of Angus Macleod. Rev. Robert Finlayson said of Angus, "This poor, witless man could claim more spiritual children in the parish of Lochs than all the ministers who preached there in that generation. Although he was little removed from absolute idiocy his blessed Lord was to him a daily companion with whom he conversed with all the reality of a present visible person. Night and day his love for perishing men was his continual theme, and all who met him had to answer the question: Do you love the Lord Jesus Christ?'" (13)

Angus Macleod of Uig was known as "Aonghas nam beann", "Angus of the Hills." His father was a shepherd and they lived in a little cottage in the hills. Angus did not possess much intellectual fiber. He never learned the alphabet. His teacher said he could never get past the letter, "B". He never learned to read or to do math. In trying to learn to read, Angus always said he did not see Christ in the letters.

Angus was converted to Christ during the Uig Revival. He became so in tune of the Kingdom of God that Christ became his whole desire. Angus was a simpleton. He could never count the fingers on his hand, but when he was once asked how God was three in one, he made three folds of his pant leg, and then stretched them into one. (14)

Once, Angus applied to his Minister, Alexander Macleod, for the privilege of sitting at the Lord's Table at Communion. Macleod refused him on the ground of intellectual incapacity. Angus felt as if the door of heaven had been slammed shut against him. Some believe that the Session later relented and allowed Angus to come to the Lord's Table.

Angus, although his mind was weak, lived more in the world of the invisible than of the visible. The things of the spiritual world were far more real to him than the things of this world.. Angus lived in a world of his own. He would talk to the Lord as he walked. People would pass Angus and hear him talking to the Lord. One day, Angus was overheard praying, "Oh, my Savior, the Black One came to me today. He was going to trouble me. Fire was in his eye. I told him You were coming and I expected You soon. Oh, You should see how he took to his heels." (15)

Angus was in great demand to pray at church. When he prayed, it was as if heaven opened. One day he was asked to pray, but Angus declined. They insisted that he pray. Again, Angus declined. A man said, "Angus, Jonah prayed when he was worse off than you. He prayed when he was in the Whale's belly." Angus replied, "Ah! But I have the whale in mine today!" (16)

Angus died while on a trip to a Communion Season on the Isle of Skye. He is buried in a cemetery on Skye, where there is not even a piece of wood to mark his grave.

MALCOLM MACLEOD- In 1834, Malcolm was 95 years of age. His daughter brought home notes of a sermon she had heard at church. Through the notes of this sermon, Malcolm was converted to Christ. His whole nature was changed. He spent hours in prayer and praise. Alexander Macleod, the

Minister, came to his bedside and preached to him on the man who lay for 38 years at the pool of Bethesda. When the Communion Season came, four friends carried Malcolm to church, and placed him at the Lord's Table. The crowd was deeply moved. As he sat at the Lord's Table, Alexander Macleod said, "He is a most interesting sight, caught at the eleventh hour. O how wonderful are the ways of sovereign grace!" (17)

KITTY SMITH- Catherine (Kitty) Smith lived with her family on the Island of Pabbay in the middle of Loch Roag. This small island lies off the coast close by the village of Uig. Only seven families lived on the island. There was something unusual about Kitty from her early childhood. She had a spiritual nature that most people would not understand.

When Kitty was two years of age, she could be seen laying aside her toys, clasping her hands together and praying. When she was three, she would quote the 23rd Psalm with fervor. Her parents taught her the Lord's Prayer, which they would hear her saying in the middle of the night. When she was six years of age, Kitty and the other children were out herding the cattle. Kitty began to speak to them of the beauty of Christ. On one occasion, her mother saw Kitty staring intently into a roaring fire. Her mother asked what she was doing. Kitty replied, "I am seeing that my state would be awful if I were to fall into that fire, even though I should be immediately taken out, but, woe is me, those who are cast into hell fire will never come out again." (18)

When Kitty was seven years of age, she contracted a deadly disease which ended her life on earth. She knew she was dying. Her father asked Kitty whom she pitied most of those she was leaving behind. Kitty said, "I pity everyone who is in a Christ-less state." Toward the end, Kitty prayed, "Oh,

Holy One of Israel, save me from death. Oh, redeem me from death." In her last few moments, her father leaned over her bed, and asked, "Kitty, where are you now?" Kitty replied, "I am on the shore." (19) And, with those words, Kitty Smith entered Glory!

JOHN MACDONALD- John Macdonald has come down in the history of the Church of Scotland as "The Apostle of the North." He is, perhaps, the greatest evangelist the Scottish Highlands and the Hebrides Islands has ever known.

Macdonald was born on November 12, 1779 in Sutherland. A neighbor widow was present to help at the birth. And, this widow, after John was weaned, insisted on taking him to her own house. For five years John was in the care of this widow. Every night the widow would kneel beside John and pray for him. So deep were the impressions on the mind of young John that in his last years he could still repeat some of her prayers.

John Macdonald was licensed to preach in 1805, and ordained as a missionary preacher in 1806. He became the Minister of the Gaelic Church in Edinburgh in 1807, and, while at this church, Macdonald went through an important change in his life, which he referred to as a "fresh baptism of the Holy Spirit."

Macdonald became Minister of a church in Urquhart in 1813. Then, he moved to Ferintosh in Ross-shire. In his first year at Ross-shire, his wife died. Within a few days of her death, Communion Season was due to be celebrated in his church. His elders expected him to cancel the Communion Services, but Macdonald said to them, "No, let not the death of my wife interfere with commemorating the death of my Savior." (20) At the Communion, 10,000 people were present to hear Macdonald preach on the text, "I will betroth thee unto me forever" (Hosea 2:19).

Macdonald preached on the Isle of Skye, and in 1827 he was going to the small island of St. Kilda to preach and to help build a church. The storms would not allow the boat to dock at St. Kilda, and, returning to Harris, Macdonald made his way to Uig in time for the first Communion Season at the Uig Church since Alexander Macleod had become Minister. A huge crowd of 9,000 to 11,000 people crowded the hillside to listen to the "Wild man of Ferintosh." The blessings were many, and revival was the aftermath.

In 1842, Macdonald returned to the Isle of Skye to preach. He conducted a Communion Service at Snizort where 12,000 to 15,000 attended, and hundreds of people fell down as if they were dead.

On returning home from Skye, Macdonald stopped to preach at Invermoriston. One man who was present said, "He preached with great power, from the words of Paul to the Philippian jailer. The impression of that day was extraordinary. The place was like a battlefield strewed with the dead and dying. Not a few survived who testify that the Lord was, of a truth, present that day." (21)

John Macdonald, the Apostle of the North, died at the age of 70, in 1849. Those who heard him preach through the years were always deeply impressed concerning three things in his preaching; the prominence he gave to the glory of the Person of Christ, the freeness of the way of salvation, and the way he described justification by faith in Christ alone.

FINLAY COOK- During the time of the Uig Revival of 1824-29, the northern part of the Isle of Lewis was under the total domination of moderatism. The areas of Knock, Cross, and Ness had slumbered in spiritual darkness for years and years. In 1829, Finlay Cook assumed the pastorate of the church in the Parish of Ness. He served in this capacity for four years. When the spiritual awakening occurred in Uig , it began to reach out and touch every parish on the island. The revival which came to the northern end of the island had two characteristics, one physical and the other spiritual. Some of the people who came under the power of the Holy Spirit would fall forward into a faint. Others had the power to make prophecies about the future. Finlay Cook had a fear that nervous excitement might be mistaken for the power of God, so he became very careful to discountenance all physical demonstrations. Cook preached with power, rich, doctrinal sermons. One Christian lady said that R. Finlayson of Lochs was the most affecting preacher she had ever heard; John Macrae the most searching; Dr. John Kennedy the nearest to God in prayer, but Finlay Cook was the most evangelical.

Finlay Cook left Lewis in 1833, and became Minister of the church in Inverness.

JOHN MACRAE- John Macrae was born in 1794 in Kintail on the mainland of Scotland. When a young man, he listened to the prayer of Finlay Munro as he blessed the food before a meal, and became stricken in his heart about his need of God. A while later, he heard a sermon preached by John Macdonald of Ferintosh, the "Apostle of the North."The sermon was from the Song of Solomon 3: 11, "Go forth, O ye daughters of Zion, and see King Solomon with the crown with which his mother crowned him on the day of his wedding, the day of the gladness of his heart." Macrae went home in deep distress of soul. His biographer, Mr. Macmaster said, "His distress of mind was for a time extreme, unfitting him for the ordinary duties of life......When his foot struck against a clod or stone on the hillside, he fell helplessly to the ground. Many in the district thought he must have lost his reason." (22) At the Communion Season at Ferintosh, Macrae found peace with God through the Lord Jesus Christ.

Macrae became a teacher. He made his way to Uig on the Isle of Lewis, . Alexander Macleod made him one of the Gaelic teachers, and Macrae was present when the glory of God fell on Uig. On one occasion, Alexander Macleod asked Macrae to deliver a message to the congregation on Communion Sabbath at Uig. As Macrae stood to speak, Robert Finlayson of Lochs said, "Wait now till you hear how he will make chaff of all we have been saying here today." (23)

When Finlay Cook left the pastorate of Ness in 1833, John Macrae was ordained and assumed the pastorate of that church for six years. In 1839, he moved to the church at Knockbain on the mainland of Scotland. It was while he was at Knockbain that he acquired the nickname, "MacRath Mor", "Big Macrae." This was a reference to his large frame. Since that day, John Macrae was, and still is today, called MacRath Mor.

In 1849, Macrae became Minister of the Gaelic Church, Greenock, Scotland where he labored until 1857. He accepted a call to the church in Lochs, Lewis. Because of the large size of the congregation, and his failing health, Macrae moved, in 1866, to the church in Carloway, Lewis. In 1871, he resigned the church because of ill health, and went home to glory in 1876.

What about John Macrae as a preacher? He was one of the most powerful preachers in the Northern Highlands. His huge size, voice like thunder, and his strong grasp of scriptural theology gained the immediate attention of his hearers. He was noted for his minute preparation in his sermons, although he did not write out a manuscript, but carried with him into the pulpit a bare outline of what he wanted to say.

As an example, in one of his sermons on sin, and Christ

dying for that sin, Macrae said, "They shall look upon Him Whom they have pierced. Every sin has its own sting, and every sting in every sin for which Christ suffered entered His very soul. There is one sin, however, of such dread persistency, and of which it might be said that it has two stings. It is like the sharp piercing blades of shears which are joined in the one handle. This is the sin of unbelief. With that sin many seek to strike the Son of God in glory under the fifth rib." (24)

Not only is John Macrae (MacRath Mor) remembered for his spiritual power in the pulpit, but he is also remembered for his deep compassion for people. When he was Minister of the Ness Church on Lewis, he visited a godly man who lived on the east side of the island. Macrae knew that the man was poor, but when he arrived at the home, he found the man, Angus Graham, eating a small bit of bread and drinking water. This was all the food he had. Macrae made a comment about the meagerness of his meal. Angus Graham told Macrae that he had what the Lord had promised, and all of His blessings besides. When Macrae returned to his home, he saw his table covered with food. He would not take a bite until he had sent most of it to Angus Graham. (25)

ANGUS MACIVER- Angus was born in 1799 in the small village of Reef, in the parish of Uig, Isle of Lewis. His father was a fisherman, and Angus grew up in a family of ten children. Although he was never a church minister, Angus Maciver became one of the leading figures in the Uig Revival, and in other revival movements on the Isle of Lewis, and the mainland of Scotland.

In his formative years, Maciver lived in a society where there was no form of godliness of any kind. No family worshiped God in the home. The Church Minister at Uig was ignorant of the gospel of Jesus Christ. While growing up,

Maciver never remembered the name of Christ ever being mentioned from the pulpit of the Uig Church. When the baptism of children was to be done, it was always in one of the homes of the community. After the baptism, the people would pass around a bottle of whiskey. When the Sacrament of the Lord's Supper was dispensed at the church, it was always the custom to bring plenty of whiskey to church. Before the services began, the people would sit outside drinking whiskey. They would go from the table of the drunkard to the Table of the Lord, profaning the holy ordinance of the Lord Jesus.(26)

When Maciver was 15 years of age, he had a deep desire to acquire a Gaelic Bible, and to learn to read it. He bought an Irish Psalm Book in a bookstore in Stornoway, and began memorizing the Psalms.

At the age of 20, Maciver contracted smallpox, and was very close to death for many days. During this severe illness, he had a vision of hell and his place in it. He also saw a man in beautiful apparel standing above him. The man in beautiful clothing threw him a rope. He climbed up out of sight of the pit of hell, and Maciver thanked the man in beautiful clothing for his kindness. He recovered from the smallpox still not knowing Jesus Christ. In fact, Maciver said he was in such a miserable state that he did not know he was a sinner before God, or that he needed a Savior. He said that he literally did not know the name of Christ. (27)

After his illness was over, Maciver learned that a neighbor had secured a Gaelic Bible from a friend in Stornoway, and he began going to the neighbor's house to read the Book for himself. This was his first sight of the Bible. But, he did not read it as the Word of God. To him, the Bible was a sealed book in a spiritual sense. He read it as a historical book only. Because he could read in both English and Gaelic, the next winter Maciver was hired as a teacher in the area. It was while teaching that a few of his friends told him that a man was in Stornoway hiring young men for the Hudson Bay Company to go to North America and work. He signed on for a three-year term. Seventeen of the young men of his area signed on to work for the Hudson Bay Company. Maciver was now 21 years of age.

When Maciver returned to Uig at the age of 24, he looked up his two closest friends, Peter Maclean and Malcolm Macritchie. He found that both of these men had been converted to Christ, and were now busy in the work of the Lord. He also found a new minister at the Uig Church, Alexander Macleod. Everything had changed. When he had left Uig, Rev. Munro, the Uig Minister, had, for 46 years, been following a set form of duties, but there had been no gospel, no word of hope, no message of salvation through Jesus Christ. Now, Alexander Macleod was preaching. The village of Uig, that had been a spiritually dry, parched land, now was blooming and rich in Jesus Christ. The Uig Revival of 1824-28 had come.

Maciver began to spend his time walking by the sea, praying and reading. He would come home late in the evening. Then, suddenly, a remarkable change came in the life of Angus Maciver. He was born again.

Maciver was employed to teach children in the parish. Eight young men in the church were being groomed to go to the university, and then, to enter the ministry. Maciver could never see his way clear to become a minister, but he did see his way clear to throw his life into the work of persuading sinners to be reconciled to God through the Lord Jesus Christ.

Schools were set up in the Uig region. The Uig minister, Alexander Macleod, planted teachers in these schools. Many of these teachers later became ministers; John Macrae (MacRath Mor), John Finlayson, Peter Maclean, Malcolm Macritchie, Alexander MacColl, and John MacQueen. Angus Maciver was also one of these teachers, but never became a minister. He spent his life as a teacher, teaching the Word of God to the common people.

Maciver's first appointment was with the Gaelic School Society. He was sent to Ardnamurchan in Argyle on the mainland of Scotland. After three years, he was transferred to a village three miles south of Inveraray. In both of these positions, Maciver was brought up on charges by the local church ministers. In both instances, the church ministers had no sympathy with his zeal and evangelical beliefs. Two charges were brought against him; that he was holding services during regular worship hours, and he was preaching. When the Presbytery ordered him to stop doing these things, Maciver replied, "You may stop my salary, but you cannot shut my lips." (28)

Mrs. Augusta Mackenzie, whose sister owned the Isle of Lewis, took an interest in Angus Maciver. She built him a house and a meeting house at Back, seven miles north of Stornoway. She continued supporting him until the end of her life. At this time, the people of Back were expected to walk to Stornoway and worship on Sunday. Maciver began to teach and lecture in the meeting house Mrs. Mackenzie had built. Large crowds of young and old began to come. Because of the long trip to Stornoway, the people began to come on weekdays and on Sunday to hear this layman, Angus Maciver, teach the Word of God. A spiritual revival took place that changed this part of the Isle of Lewis forever.

Again, Maciver was brought before the Presbytery on charges of holding services at Back during regular worship hours, and not appearing with the people of Back in the parish church of Stornoway on Sunday.

The Presbytery came to a compromise. They told Maciver that if he would come with the people to the church in Stornoway at the hours of worship, then go home, a walk of 14 miles total, he could then hold his own meeting at Back. He gave this answer, "If a man was hungry, and needed food, would it be a right thing for them to ask him to go to the Manse of Tongue for it when there was nothing there but the bare walls?" The Stornoway Minister, Mr. Cameron, asked, "Do you mean I am not preaching the gospel?" Maciver replied, "If you do, I can not find it in your preaching." (29)

Alexander Macleod, the minister at Uig, arranged for Angus Maciver to come to the Island of Bernera, a small island off the southwest coast of Lewis. He appointed him as a teacher and missionary. The Island of Bernera is four miles in length and two miles wide. The climate was devastating to Maciver, who suffered from asthma. During the week he taught the young people English and Gaelic. On Sunday he preached to the people in the middle of the day, and again at night.

One of the wonderful attributes of Maciver was his beautiful singing voice. On one occasion when the Uig Revival was at its height, John Macdonald of Ferintosh, the "Apostle of the North" was present. Angus Maciver was leading the singing outside. In the middle of a song, suddenly a godly, divine impression moved over the people. They bowed their heads and began to weep. The singing almost stopped. The only two still singing were John Macdonald and Angus Maciver. Many people were gloriously saved that day.

Maciver stayed on the Island of Bernera for eighteen years, teaching and telling the story of Jesus Christ. The people of Bernera would come to the meeting house for the night services carrying lighted peat with tongs, and a fresh supply of peat under their arms. There were no lanterns, no paraffin oil. A few families had candles, and there were a few lamps in which they used fish oil. But the main source of heat and light was a peat fire.

Angus Maciver was working on the Island of Bernera when the Great Disruption of 1843 occurred. He, along with almost all the people of Bernera, left the established Church of Scotland and went with the Free Church movement.

Soon after the Disruption of 1843, Alexander Macleod left the Uig Church and became Minister of the church in Lochalsh on the mainland of Scotland. Maciver returned to Back as Catechist, and in charge of the Free Church there.

Because of severe attacks of Asthma, he was sent to Maryburgh, a small town on the mainland of Scotland, where he remained for the rest of his life. At Maryburgh, his health improved, and he began teaching and preaching in the school house. The meetings began to overflow. During the summer months, crowds would stand outside. Maciver's last days were filled with deep sorrow. A son died at the age of 21, and a daughter passed away, then in March, 1856, another daughter died of high fever. During her illness, Maciver contracted the fever also. He could not go to his daughter's funeral. He walked beside her coffin from the bedroom to the top of the stairs, put his hand on the coffin and told his daughter, goodbye, and that he would see her soon. He turned from the head of the stairs, went to his bed, from which he never arose. Angus Maciver died eleven days later on October 2, 1856 at the age of 57.

Angus Maciver, singer, Bible teacher, preacher, friend of sinners, made a deep and lasting impression on the Uig

Revival of 1824-28.

FINLAY MUNRO

Finlay Munro was born in the Tain area of Scotland. After his conversion, he began his career as a Gaelic teacher. Soon he developed a passion to be an evangelist. He began preaching, which brought him much sorrow and trouble. He was a lay-preacher, and in that day, a lay-preacher was looked upon with much suspicion. Only those who had been properly schooled and approved were to preach.

Munro made two trips to the Isle of Lewis. His first trip was probably in the year 1818. He came by boat to the northern end of the island at Ness. He preached down the eastern coast of Lewis, in Ness, North Tolsta, Stornoway, Back and Gress. It is quite possible that Munro was a very young man at this time. The people called him, "Am balach leis a'Bhiobull", "The boy with the Bible." (30)

While preaching in Gress, Malcolm Macleod was converted to Christ. In later years, Macleod stood in a church meeting, and spoke concerning that time of his conversion. Macleod said, "When I was young in Lewis, word came to the village one day that a service was to be held by a lad who was going about with a Bible. As the others were going to the service, I followed them, and sat on the outer circle of the congregation. As the boy began to preach, I became so enthralled by his teaching that I could not hold back the tears. As he went on, I edged nearer and nearer to him, until at last I had shed a bowl-full of tears, and found myself at his feet. The work that began in my heart that day has not yet stopped, nor will it stop." (31)

On this first trip to Lewis, Munro made his way further south to Balallan and to Harris. The people, in general, welcomed him with open hearts, but some of the people and some ministers were extremely hostile to him, and his preaching.

Munro made his final trip to Lewis after 1824. It was in 1824 that Alexander Macleod was installed as minister in Uig. Macleod was very much opposed to the preaching of Munro. On this final trip, Munro preached in Shader, Barvas, Callanish, and Breasclete. He felt a strong desire to preach in Glen Valtos. While preaching in Glen Valtos, Alexander Macleod attended one of the services at the urging of a dear lady who was a member of his congregation at Uig. When the service was concluded, Alexander Macleod came to Munro to tell him good-bye. He asked Munro if he had a snuff- box. Munro replied that he did, and he handed his stuff-box to Macleod. Alexander Macleod put a pound sterling in the stuff-box and handed it back to Munro. (32)

When Finley Munro was ready to leave the Isle of Lewis for the last time, he announced that he would hold a final service on Muirneag. This is a hill about 800 feet high, and located four miles from the nearest village. A large crowd gathered for this final service. If you go to Lewis today, the spot where Finley Munro stood to preach that day is marked, and is called, "Tom Fhionnlaigh", "Finley's Knoll." That final sermon of Munro's was from Isaiah 25:6-9. "And in this mountain the Lord of hosts will make for all people a feast of choice pieces, a feast of wines on the lees, of fat things full of marrow, of well-refined wines on the lees. And He will destroy on this mountain the surface of the covering cast over all people, and the veil that is spread over all nations. He will swallow up death forever, and the Lord God will wipe away tears from all faces; the rebuke of His people He will take away from all the earth; for the Lord has spoken. And it will be said in that day; behold, this is our God; we have waited for Him, and He will save us. This is the Lord; we have waited for Him; we will be glad and rejoice in His salvation."

Finley Munro died in 1834. In his last years, his mind began to deteriorate. This "boy with the Bible" was laid to rest in Tain, the place of his birth.

JOHN MORRISON

Although I am calling it the Isle of Lewis, the island is made up of two geographical areas, called by different names. Some books list the official name of this island," Lewis on Harris", or "Lewis and Harris." The northern end of the island is called Lewis, while the southern end of the island is named Harris. Lewis and Harris share a common ancestry. A Norse Clan named Leod inhabited the island. Two sons of Leod, therefore named Macleod, each founded a clan. The son, Torquil, founded the Macleods of Lewis, and the son, Tormod, founded the Macleods of Harris.

Lewis and Harris are different historically, geographically, and culturally. The northern part of the island, Lewis, is flat, no trees, an endless expanse of peat bogs and heather. The southern part of the island, Harris, is filled with mountains and lochs (lakes).

In 1790, John Morrison was born in Rodil, a village of Harris. Morrison was entirely self-educated, and could write in English, Gaelic and Latin. He worked as a blacksmith for twenty-three years. Morrison had a deep spiritual longing in his soul that he could find no way to satisfy. In 1821, he wrote a poem which spoke of his longing for a higher spiritual life. At this time, Morrison was very conscious that he was a sinner, but he said he was seeking "The Unknown God."

That same year, 1821, Rev. John Macdonald, the Apostle

of the North, visited Harris during the month of September. Morrison went to hear him preach. He was so intrigued that he went back a second time. On that night, Macdonald preached on the text, "This is a faithful saying, and worthy of all acceptation, that Christ Jesus came into the world to save sinners; of whom I am chief" (I Timothy 1:15). That night, John Morrison was converted to Christ. The Unknown God became the Known Redeemer for him.

Morrison began his Christian witness in conversations with different people. He then began prayer meetings in his home. People started streaming to his home for these meetings. Many were intrigued, some were suspicious. As time went by, Morrison went out of his own home to other villages, carrying the good news of Christ. Many opposed his teaching. Some heaped slander on him. Finally, in 1830, Morrison held an open-air meeting in Tarbert, Harris, and over 2,000 attended this meeting. Revival had come to Harris. Meetings were held every night, except Saturday, and three meetings were held on Sunday. When the meetings were concluded, the people would wander off, alone, to the seashore where they would pour out prayers to the Lord. The little children stopped playing their children games, and were seen in the fields, praying to the Lord of heaven.

In 1830, Dr. Macdonald, the Apostle of the North, came back to Harris. A man came to John Morrison's blacksmith shop to tell him of the return of Macdonald. Morrison said, "Someone came one evening to the smithy, where I was hard at work at the anvil, and mentioned that Dr. Macdonald had come. I tried to subdue my emotions and longed for the absence of the messenger. When he had gone, I ran to the smithy door and bolted it. I could then, when alone, give scope to these emotions. I danced for joy, danced round and round the smithy floor; for I felt a load suddenly taken off my spirit. I danced until I felt fatigued; and I then knelt down, and prayed and gave thanks." (33)

Morrison strictly observed the Sabbath. He believed that it was a day to keep holy unto the Lord. He would not allow any bread to be sliced with a knife. Any dishes that were washed by a servant on the Sabbath, he would order them to be put outside, and they were never used again.

John Morrison lived to see great revival come to the southern end of the island. He saw spiritual awakening. He died in the village of Leacli, Harris, in his sleep, in 1852, and was buried in Rodil, the village of his birth.

ALEXANDER MACLEOD- In closing this chapter on the Uig Revival of 1824-28, I find myself once again turning to the ministry of Alexander Macleod. No preacher on the Isle of Lewis was ever used in a more glorious way than this man. He came to a land devoid of true gospel purity, a people who had no understanding of the things of God, no knowledge of the work of our Lord Jesus Christ. God took this man and turned the whole Island of Lewis into a Kingdom of God on earth.

When Alexander Macleod left the Isle of Lewis, he left behind a multitude of people who held a special place in their hearts for him. It was not a matter of hero-worship, but a simple love of a people for a simple servant of God, who had done his duty.

The preaching of Alexander Macleod was straightforward, earnest, and dwelt on four main subjects; the glory of the Person of Christ, the virtue and efficacy of the sufferings of Christ, the absolute perfection of the finished righteousness of Christ, and God's great, eternal love for sinners. With these four main subjects, Alexander Macleod saw an entire island of people turned to Jesus Christ. The revivals of coming years on the Isle of Lewis are only crops that have been reaped because of the first-fruits of the revival in the village of Uig in 1824-28.

I thought much about the wisdom of placing in this work one of Alexander Macleod's sermons. I first thought it would take up too much space, but, as I read his sermon, I became convinced that one could never understand the preacher without knowing his preaching.

A SERMON BY ALEXANDER MACLEOD

"For God so loved the world that he gave His only begotten Son, that whosoever believeth in Him should not perish but have everlasting life." (John 3:16)

In these blessed words of our Lord we have the sum of the whole volume of inspiration, a most wonderful display of divine love, a most glorious intelligence and glad tidings of joy to all people. Nicodemus, a Pharisee and ruler of the Jews, struck with the indications of supernatural powers and authority, which were manifested in our Savior's miracles, acknowledged his conviction of His divine mission, and immediately came to Him to receive instruction, and there are two things on which our Lord chiefly insists in this discourse on this interesting occasion. He first teaches him the necessity of regeneration, next the medium through which salvation was to be accomplished, and the indispensable necessity of believing in Him in order to have eternal life, and as he was discoursing with a master in Israel. He illustrates this great subject by a fact recorded in their law, and which prefigured the Redeemer's death, that as Moses lifted up the serpent in the wilderness, even so the Son of Man must be lifted up on the cross, that whosoever believeth on Him should not perish but have everlasting life, and that he might divest him of that self-righteousness so peculiar to the Jewish people and so congenial to the human mind, and on which he so much founded his salvation. Our Lord further shows him that in the economy of grace everything of this kind is superseded for that as the mission of the Eternal Son of God into this world had for its object to bestow eternal life upon those who were ready to perish, so the only way of enjoying the blessing was by faith in the testimony that God has given of His Son, and as this faith is not of ourselves but the free gift of God, so the bestowment of it on men of every character and description corresponds with the grace which appeared in the Father's sending His only begotten Son into the world that whosoever believeth should not perish but have everlasting life.

In discoursing from these words, I propose in the first place, to consider the properties of God's love to a guilty and lost world; secondly, the evidence He gave of His love, He gave His only begotten Son; thirdly, the end or design of this unspeakable gift of love, that whosoever believeth on Him should not perish but have everlasting life; and, lastly, conclude with a short application.

I. The love of God is the brightest beam of divinity that ever illuminated the creation. There is an unfathomable depth in it which even the penetration of angels cannot reach, an ineffable excellence which even celestial eloquence cannot fully express.

(1) It is pure, unmixed love in its nature, object, and operation. It comprehends the various forms of divine beneficence- goodness that extends its bounties to innumerable ranks of creatures, and diffuses happiness through the various regions of the universe- grace, which so richly showers its blessings upon the undeserving without

past merit or further compensation. Mercy, that commiserates and relieves the miserable; and peace, and long-suffering which so long tolerates insolent and provoking offenders. All this divine beneficence in its different forms towards indifferent objects shows the greatness of divine love under various names. It is gracious, merciful, patient, and longsuffering love, love variegated, overflowing, and unbounded. Is not divine love displayed in the creation of this world, so well accommodated and so richly furnished for the sustenance and comfort of its inhabitants, and in rendering them capable of receiving streams of happiness from the immense fountain of divine goodness? It is by the love of God that this universe is preserved in order and harmony from age to age, and its numerous inhabitants supplies with every good thing. But is it not most conspicuously displayed as an unspeakably great, rich, free, and unmerited love in the gift of His Son to a guilty world? Almighty love, which brought the Lord of Glory from the celestial throne to die upon a cross, an atoning sacrifice for the sins of the world, in order to fit us for the incorruptible inheritance, and then to perpetuate our bliss through an eternal duration. Behold, then, what manner of love the Father hath bestowed upon us that we should be called the sons of God, a subject so very grand and so elevating that our limited capacities are quite inadequate to comprehend it. Who can by searching find it out? Who can trace it to perfection? It is as high as heaven. What can we do, deeper than hell what can we know? Surely the measure thereof is longer than the earth and broader than the sea. But while this eternal love of God is an unfathomable ocean, we adore the God of our salvation, who sheds it abroad in the hearts of His people by the Holy Spirit, that they with all saints may be able to comprehend in some degree what is the breadth and length and depth and height, and to know the love of Christ, which passeth knowledge. For though creation be replete with evident traces of the goodness and love of God, yet it is the work of redemption that gives the most exalted display of this most animating and delightful truth. Accordingly, when the Lord promised to make a New Covenant with the house of Israel, He intimated that he would therein carry the demonstration of it far beyond whatever could be conceived of it either in creation or providence. I will make an everlasting covenant with them (says He) that I will not turn away from them to do them good. Yea, I will rejoice over them to do them good, and will bring upon them all the good that I have promised them, and my people shall be satisfied with my goodness, saith the Lord. And He gives us this as the amount of the whole, They shall be my people, and I will be their God.' The highest possible display of His love was manifested when He gave His Son to die to procure our redemption, the just for the unjust, that he might bring us unto God. For in this He at once commended His love to us as unspeakable, that while we were yet sinners, Christ died for the ungodly, in order to redeem them from sin, death, and hell. To teach them the revelations of His will and the declaration of His promises, in His determination to sanctify and to glorify them, in supporting them through life, blessing them in death, and bringing them to glory. When we, therefore, consider the unspeakable highness and holiness of our heavenly Father, and the lowness and wretchedness of those on whom He conferred His unspeakable gift, we are constrained to exclaim with the inspired writer, God is Love.'

(2) It is an everlasting love. The Lord' says the prophet Jeremiah, appeared of old unto me, saying, Yea, I loved thee with an everlasting love, and therefore with loving kindness

have I drawn thee.' Blessed be the God and Father of our Lord Jesus Christ,' exclaimed the illustrious apostle, who hath blessed us with all spiritual blessings in Christ Jesus according as He has chosen us in Him before the foundation of the world, that we should be holy and without blame before Him in love.' O, the matchless love of our God to a whole world full of ignorance, carnality, and enmity, against His holy perfections, in a state of actual rebellion against Him, and without the least desire ever to know, serve, or enjoy Him. Yet, hear, O heavens, and be astonished O earth, God loved this world of perishing sinners. But how much no tongue can tell, for eye hath not seen, nor ear heard, neither hath it entered into the heart of man what things the Lord prepared for them that love Him. It is so unspeakable and so unlike anything in human affairs that our text makes no comparison in order to describe it. It has no parallel or similitude among men, and, therefore, it is only said, God so loved the world that he gave us His Son. In most cases human love is expressed by words more than by deeds, but the love of God is such that it cannot be fully expressed by words. It is a divine contrivance which we, while in this tabernacle, cannot fully comprehend.

(3) It is an immutable love, as in Malachi 3:6, For I am the Lord, I change not, therefore ye sons of Jacob are not consumed.' He will rest in His love towards His people, for His love is engaged for their everlasting security. Having made them the objects of His free love, a primary fruit of His eternal favor, this love must abate, and His purposes must be rendered void before they are left to themselves. But if the Lord of hosts has purposed, who shall disannul it? If His hands be stretched out to execute His designs, who shall turn it back, before He has accomplished the end He has determined? As He thought, so shall it come to pass. As He

purposed, so shall it stand. He has set His delight on the sons of men, and, therefore, He rests. He takes the highest complacency in the exercise of His love towards all His favorite objects. He rejoices over them with singing, and takes a divine pleasure in doing them good. So firmly did the illustrious Apostle believe this salutary truth that he exulted in the contemplation of God's immutable love, expressing himself in the following forcible and pathetic language: For I am persuaded that neither death, nor life, nor angels, nor principalities, nor powers, nor things present, nor things to come, nor height, nor depth, nor any other creature shall be able to separate us from the love of God which is in Christ Jesus our Lord.'

(4) It is a free love, as nothing out of God Himself can be the cause of it, for then there would be a cause prior to Him. The misery of the creature is not the cause of it, for He is not wrought upon as creatures are, nor are the merits of the creature the cause. Not by works of righteousness which we have done, but according to His mercy, He saved us by the washing of regeneration and renewing of the Holy Ghost. It is, therefore, free, as it arises from His sovereign will and pleasure through the merits of our Redeemer. Let us then consider the freeness of this love, and rejoice in the exercise of faith and lively hope that the most glorious day shall soon arrive when our happy anticipations of His immediate presence shall be unspeakably realized, and when we shall see Him as he is.

II. The evidence of God's love to sinners. He gave us His only begotten Son.

(1) Then, we have the clearest evidence of this love in the Incarnation of our Lord. Here the unspeakable gift of God, manifested in the flesh, is most conspicuously displayed to a fallen race. Now, the original promise made to our first parents is fully realized. The God and Savior of Abraham, Isaac, and Jacob, to the great astonishment of men and angels, condescended to appear in the likeness of sinful flesh, and now the divine predictions are amply fulfilled, For unto us a child is born, unto us a son is given, and the government shall be upon His shoulders, and His name shall be called Wonderful, Counselor, the mighty God, the everlasting Father, the Prince of Peace.' How clearly did He manifest His love to us in the humiliation and sufferings of our Lord, in the poverty of His birth, the reproach of His character, the pains of His body, the power of His enemies, the desertion of His friends, the weight of His peoples' sins, the slow, ignominious, and painful nature of His death, and the hiding of His Father's face, for He hath made Him sin for us who knew no sin, that we might be made the righteousness of God in Him. And the Lord hath laid upon Him the iniquity of us all.' Yet some have impiously asserted that the sufferings of Christ were only in appearance and not in reality. But if hunger and thirst, if revilings and contempt, if condemnation and crucifixion be sufferings, our Lord suffered; if the sinless infirmities of our nature, if the weight of our sins, if the malice of men, if the machinations of Satan, if the hand of God could make Him suffer, our Savior suffered. If the annals of time, if the writings of His Apostles, if the death of His martyrs, if the confession of Gentiles, if the scoffs of the Jews be testimonies, our Lord suffered. He, therefore, that spared not His only

begotten Son, but delivered Him up for us all, how shall He not with Him, also, freely give us all things. This great doctrine, therefore, of the remission of sins through the expiatory sacrifice of our Lord is that in which we can behold the great and mysterious love of God, and is the doctrine which stands as it were in the very face of the divine oracles, and claims our preeminent regard. It is this which impresses the Christian dispensation with so gracious and merciful a character, and justly gives it the designation of glad tidings. Though every part of our Lord's obedience was meritorious and tended to magnify the law, yet His death upon the cross was its perfection and consummation; then it was that He exclaimed, 'It is finished.' In that tremendous hour He satisfied the penal demands of justice, He silenced the thunders of Mount Sinai, He conquered death, He triumphed over principalities and the powers of darkness, and opened the gates of everlasting life to sinners, dark and cloudy as that day appeared to the eye of sense, it was the brightest day that ever shone upon a guilty world, for on that day a light above the brightness of the firmament shone through the whole Jewish economy. Types met with their antitype, shadows were turned into substance, victims no longer bled upon the smoking altars. The veil of the temple was rent in twain, and a new order of things rose before us. Whilst infidelity triumphed and insulted our dying Lord, saying, He saved others, Himself He cannot save,' it spoke indeed the truth. He was enchained and bound, but it was by a love to us and our salvation. Thus we read He was cut off out of the land of the living for the transgression of my people was He stricken, for it pleased God the Father to bruise Him and put Him to grief, and in this he commended His love most conspicuously toward us that while we were yet sinners Christ died for us.

III. The end or design of this gift of love was that whosoever believeth on Him should not perish but have everlasting life. This was God's great object in giving His Son to be the propitiation for our sins. He has not sent Him into the world to condemn the world, as sinners might have expected, but that the world might be saved by Him. In this blessed design of man's redemption we behold the three divine persons moved by sovereign and free love, heartily joining in the most wonderful scheme of our everlasting salvation, the blessed Father to exert the grace, the Son to advance the merit, the Holy Ghost to apply the purchased benefits, the Father to adopt us for His children, the Son to redeem us for His mystical members, and the Holy Ghost to sanctify and renew our hearts. The design of this unspeakable gift is no less manifested in the resurrection of our Lord, when He secured the union of His people as His quickened and mystical members and their resurrection to everlasting life. It is no less conspicuous in His ascension when He took possession of heaven in their name, prepares them for the heavenly mansions, pours down His Spirit upon them for that end, weans their affection from transitory objects, and attracts them to things above where He is, making continual intercession on their behalf, and securing their exaltation in due time. It was in the consideration of this grand truth that the Apostle Paul spoke of the great Mystery of Godliness, God was manifest in the flesh, justified in the spirit, seen of angels, preached unto the Gentiles, believed on in the world, and received up into glory. All which was intended to adopt us into His family to sanctify our nature and receive us into glory, and when we consider the despicable objects on whom this unmerited favor was conferred, we are devoutly struck with unspeakable and holy veneration of the Divine Author, from whom all this has originated freely. When men adopt it is on account of some excellency in the persons adopted, as Pharaoh's daughter adopted Moses, because he was exceeding fair; and Mordecai adopted Esther because she was his uncle's daughter and exceeding fair. But man has nothing in him which merits this divine act, as in Ezekiel 16:5, None eye pitied thee to do any of these things unto thee, to have compassion on thee, but thou wast cast out in the open field to the loathing of thy person in the day that thou wast born.' It was in this state our Maker found us, when He said, Live,' and when He pours His Holy Spirit on His people they receive Christ by faith as freely offered in the gospel to this end. His divine grace is imparted to them in order to excite their gratitude and direct their attention to the glory of Him who called them from darkness to His marvelous light to accomplish the great end of their salvation. They are divinely conducted to run the Christian race with faith, hope, and love; they proceed in their journey towards the heavenly Jerusalem, faith is the foundation and measure of hope. The latter is only the anticipation of those blessings which the former realizes and presents to the mind. If faith be strong, hope is full of immortality and glory. Her heavenly prospects vary with the divine principle from which she proceeds. She is associated also with that humility which waits with patience for the full accomplishment of the promises. Hence, as an anchor within the veil, she keeps the soul sure and steadfast amidst all the fluctuating tides and tempests of this lower world. But these graces, however important, beneficial, and permanent in their effects, are only instrumental to that grace of love with which we shall ever be filled in everlasting praises of Him who loved us. All other graces are but means to this blessed end. When we enter into a state of grace the full fruition of God, even eternal life, is ultimately intended. The end of God's unspeakable gift and all the graces of His Spirit through Him are to land us at last in the unfading and incorruptible inheritance. Love should adorn our Christian profession while here below, The end of the commandment is charity out of a pure heart and of a good conscience, and faith unfeigned.' 'Now abideth faith, hope, and charity, these three; but the greatest of these is charity.' It is of a superior and transcendent nature, without it all other gifts are but as sounding brass and tinkling cymbals. While faith is that primary grace which apprehends and appropriates the salvation of Christ, and while hope ardently looks for the perfect and ultimate fruition of this salvation, divine love is that holy affection which constitutes the health and felicity of the soul. It is the greatest evidence that we can have of being called of God. It is the prize itself, for in proportion to our love we dwell in God and God in us. Of all the Christian graces it is the most general and comprehensive, concentrating every other into its own nature. It suffereth long and is kind, without usurping the place or disturbing the functions of the rest. Love allies itself to them all, regulates their exercise, preserves their simplicity, refers them to their proper end, and by purifying the secret chambers of the soul, keeps up a hallowed flame of devotion which diffuses life and splendor over every part of divine truth, and thus maintains their just empire in the heart with a single eye to the glory of God. It is also eternal in its duration, charity never faileth; faith ere long will be lost in vision, and hope in enjoyment. Their specific operations do not extend beyond the grave. When they have conducted the Christian to the confines of a better country they consign him over to perfect love, there to arrive at the very fountain of love, from which all the streams run for the healing of perishing sinners, and join the spirits of the just in songs of everlasting praises to the Lamb that was slain and redeemed them by His blood.

I conclude with a short application. Is the love of God therefore from everlasting? Is it the great, the eternal, and absolutely free favor of God in Christ manifested in the vouchsafement of spiritual and eternal blessings to the unworthy entirely detached from all supposition of human worth and absolutely independent of any such thing as human goodness? O! then, all ye children of want and sons of wretchedness, whether Jews or Gentiles, to this inexhaustible fountain of God's free and unmerited love ye may freely come. Here the poor, the maimed, the halt, and the blind, with longing hearts and uplifted hands, big with expectations of being healed, may come with the utmost readiness, for the invitation extends to all characters and descriptions of men, and the proclamation (whosoever) is expressive of the freest favor and richest grace, including offenders of the worst characters, publishing pardon for sins of the deepest dye, and all ratified by Veracity itself. It affords sufficient encouragement to the vilest of sinners who is willing to owe his all to divine bounty, to receive the heavenly blessing, and with faith and gratitude to rejoice in the royal donation. Yes, it is the sovereign love of God that raises the poor from the dunghill and the needy from the dust, and sets them on thrones of glory, and numbers them among the princes of heaven. Happy, then, are they who are taught the infinitely marvelous, pleasant, powerful, and profitable truths of God in a manner that enlightens, draws, renews, ravishes, and sanctifies their heart. Happy they who being chargeable with every guilt and pollution, have them all washed away through the efficacious and expiatory sacrifice of their Lord, their righteousness and strength. How freely may they come to His throne of grace to receive of His love and sing in the heights of Zion. Happy His subjects who is love itself, whose laws are holy, just, and good, a perfect law of liberty, and whose whole administration is wisdom, righteousness, condescension, kindness, and love. O! Then may that blessed day hasten when time shall give place to eternity, when our transient glimmerings of His glory here issue in our being for ever with the Lord, when our beloved ordinances of His grace shall be exchanged for seeing the God of infinite love as He is, who will acknowledge us in the face of His dear Son, who is the light of the celestial mansions, our everlasting light, our God, and our eternal glory.(30)

There are several things that helped to bring about the Uig Revival of 1824-28. The ground was already being plowed before Alexander Macleod came to Uig to assume the pastorate of the Uig Church. There were four items that were uniquely used by the Holy Spirit to usher in revival. The Bible became available in the Gaelic language. People had the opportunity to learn their written language, and then to read the Book for themselves. Two books became widely read in the area of Uig, as well as across the Isle of Lewis; Richard Baxter's *Call to the Unconverted*, and Joseph Alliene's, *Alarm to the Unconverted.* The people also had access to the writings of Jonathan Edwards, the preacher of the great revival which had happened in America several years before. In the writings of Jonathan Edwards was included the testimony of his wife, Sarah. Sarah Edwards said, "I sought and obtained the full assurance of faith. I cannot find language to express how certain the everlasting love of God appeared. The everlasting mountains and hills were but shadows to it. My safety and happiness and eternal enjoyment of God's immutable love seemed as durable and unchanging as God himself. Melted and overcome by the sweetness of this assurance, I fell into a great flow of tears and could not forbear weeping aloud. The presence of God was so near and so real that I seemed scarcely conscious of anything else. My soul was filled and overwhelmed with light and love and joy in the Holy Ghost, and seemed just ready to go away from my body. This exultation of soul subsided into a heavenly calm and rest of soul in God, which was even sweeter than what preceded it." (34)

During this time of great revival, the owner of the Isle of Lewis was the Hon. Stewart Mackenzie. His wife, Mrs. Stewart Mackenzie, was a lady that had much to do with the revival. She was totally committed to an evangelical ministry in the churches on the island. It was Mrs. Mackenzie who named Alexander Macleod to be the church minister of the Uig church. She had a deep hunger to see the glory of God come on the people of Lewis.

When revival came to Uig, and then spread to other villages across the island, it changed the complexion of the entire island. Today, Lewis is the only one of the major islands of the Hebrides that does not have a whiskey distillery. In the early 1800s, there were two distilleries on Lewis, in Ness and in Stornoway. They were licensed to Stewart Mackenzie. Both of the distilleries were closed in 1831, and were never reopened. (35) One cannot help but wonder why the distilleries closed their doors. Could it have been that revival caused such a severe lack of business, or, perhaps the distilleries closed because of the personal convictions of Stewart Mackenzie and his wife?

What brought revival to the Isle of Lewis? That is such a difficult question, but one we will examine in a later chapter. When God looked down on Lewis He saw a people in darkness, a people in an appalling state of sin, and He sent to them His love and mercy. On the Isle of Lewis there is a little hill which goes by the name of "The Hill of Two Views" (cnoc an da sheallaidh). On a clear day, one can stand on this little hill and look toward the East, and see the waters of the Minch, looking toward the west, one can see the endless, blue waters of the Atlantic Ocean. Making use of this illustration, one Lewis preacher said that at the place where the convicted sinner has the clearest sight of his sin, there also God showed him the sea of the merits of Christ's blood where his sin can be covered forever.

Praise be to our God who brought revival to the Isle of Lewis in 1824-28! Praise God for the men and women who drew near to the heavenly Father, listened to Him, and obeyed Him by carrying the message of Jesus Christ to a dark land. Praise the Lord, who came down on this place, the Isle of Lewis, THE LAND GOD CHOSE TO LOVE (An Tir a Roghnaich Dia a Ghradhachadh)

Rev. Alexander Macleod

Angus Macleod
"Angus of the Hills"

The Uig Church

John Macrae
"Macrath Mor"

Dr. John Macdonald
"Apostle of the North"

Chapter three

"THE REVIVAL OF 1840-1843"

('DUSGADH 1840-1843)

During the early 1840's, the Isle of Lewis began to once again feel the quickening breath of the Holy Spirit. It is difficult to say which of two events spurred the revival of 1840-43. It could have been a "spill-over" of the revival of 1824-28, or the revival of 1840-43 could have been connected to the Great Disruption of 1843. The Great Disruption was the point when many churches and ministers withdrew from the Church of Scotland and formed the Free Church movement. On the Isle of Lewis, all of the ministers, with the exception of two, withdrew from the Church of Scotland and joined the Free Church. Two ministers; Mr. Macrae of Barvas and Mr. Cameron of Stornoway remained in the Church of Scotland. William Macrae, the minister of the church in Barvas remained in the Church of Scotland, but sent his family out into the new Free Church movement. He stood totally alone, a church building, a manse, but no congregation. Almost the entire membership of the churches of Lewis followed the Free Church movement. On one hand, this caused a great hardship on church members and ministers, for suddenly they had no church building in which to worship, and the minister had no manse in which to live. But, on the other hand, this Disruption brought about a renewed emphasis in faith in the Living God.

The people of Lewis were very fortunate, at the time of the Great Disruption, to have as the owner of the island, Stewart Mackenzie and his wife. It was this lady who had named Alexander Macleod as minister at Uig in 1824. She had a heart for evangelicalism, so, when the Disruption came, she was quick to grant sites for new churches, manses and school houses. In 1844, the Isle of Lewis was purchased by Sir James Matheson for 190,000 pounds. He followed the same policies as Mrs. Mackenzie, and the Free Church on Lewis prospered.

When the breath of the Holy Spirit fell on the Isle of Lewis in 1840-43, it seems that the forming of the Free Church gave a liberty, a freedom in preaching the gospel of Christ. This freedom was blessed by God in sending a fresh spirit into the land. The events of revival on Lewis were not unlike those that happened at the same time on the Isle of Skye, a neighbor island to Lewis on the South.

James MacQueen, a Baptist minister, reported that between 12,000 and 15,000 people attended a communion weekend at Snizort, Skye in September, 1842, and hundreds fell down as if they were dead.(1)

Also on Skye in 1842, the Holy Spirit fell in great power at Fairy Bridge. Roderick Macleod was the preacher to crowds between five and nine thousand. Because of his black hair, Macleod was called, "Black Rory", but as the years passed, and his influence grew, he was called Mr. Rory of Snizort. The people gathered at Fairy Bridge for several months. Macleod preached from his horse, riding in a circle around the huge crowd. One eye witness to the Fairy Bridge Revival said, "The young and the old, male and female, pouring forth from all sides of the land, from hills, and valleys, villages, hamlets and the lonely hut. The surrounding waters too were covered with about fifty skiffs, like the multitudes which dotted the sea of Tiberias, in pursuit of the Lord himself when he was manifested in the flesh. Like the goings up of the Jewish tribes to the great feast at Jerusalem, was the going up of those anxious islanders to the gospel meeting at Fairy Bridge." (2)

God was also refreshing the souls of men, women and youth on the Isle of Lewis during these same years.

Great preachers held their church posts during the Revival of 1840-43; Finlay Cook, John Macrae, John Finlayson, Donald Macrae, and Duncan Matheson. Alexander

Macleod still labored in Uig. It is interesting that immediately after the Great Disruption of 1843, Alexander Macleod left the Uig Church and moved to the church at Lochalsh on the mainland of Scotland.

One of the most unique men of this period was Kenneth Ross, a layman, whom God used mightily in awakening people. Mr. Ross was converted to Christ under the preaching of Finlay Cook, Minister of the Cross Church. He became the most popular speaker at the Friday fellowship meetings. His knowledge of Scripture was astounding. Mr. Ross had a special gift of ministering to the doubting, the afflicted and wounded. He seemed to always have a word from the Comforter to those in need.

Kenneth Ross served as Catechist in Barvas and in Carloway. Although he was a layman, he ended up with the sole charge of the church in Carloway. He was asked to take ordination and officially become a minister, but he refused. He felt that the ministry carried with it duties and responsibilities which he was not qualified to undertake.

It was in Carloway that the work of Kenneth Ross flourished. A sense of revival permeated the parish

When Kenneth Ross was on his death bed, John Macrae (Marath Mor) , who was then the minister at Lochs, came to see him. Macrae spoke of our lives here as lives of much tribulation. Kenneth Ross replied, "Mr. Macrae, it is not of my own trails and sufferings that I am thinking, but of the sufferings of my great Redeemer; on these my eyes and thoughts are set." (3)

It was while on his death bed that Mary, Kenneth Ross's second wife, said to him, "You will soon be where you will forget all your anguish." Ross replied, "Oh, I shall never forget my anguish for all eternity. It will kindle my heart to everlasting gratitude to Christ for suffering for me." (4)

The Revival of 1840-43 was borne on the Wings of the Word of God. Kenneth Ross added greatly to this as he taught the Word year after year. His gift seemed to find its great power in the Friday Night Fellowship meetings, as he expounded the Word of God with clarity and application to everyday life. The Word of God was backed up by the righteous character of his life. The Friday Fellowship Meetings had their origins in the 1600's in Ireland. Church Ministers had been driven from the churches, so church members began having Friday fellowship meetings in homes for religious communion and discussion. God used the life of Kenneth Ross in these Friday Fellowship Meetings to bring revival to Lewis.

Another Minister who had a great impact on the Revival of 1840-43 was Robert Finlayson. Finlayson was born in 1793 in Clythe. When Finlayson was baptized as a baby, the minister who baptized him said to his mother, "Take good care of this child, for you have received a Samuel from the Lord." (5)

Finlayson was tall, had brown hair and a fair complexion. His voice was so deep that it seemed to rise from the ground. He was a master of allegory, and on the Isle of Lewis, he was commonly referred to as "John Bunyan of the Highlands", or "John Bunyan Jr".

He became Minister at Lochs in 1831. The church and the manse were then in the village of Keose. At Finlayson's induction as minister at Lochs, Alexander Macleod preached the induction sermon.

Finlayson wrote an account of the parish of Lochs not long after he assumed the charge of the church. The parish stretched from Loch Seaforth to the Creed, and about ten miles inland. The parish of Lochs included the villages of Carloway and Shawbost. In his account, Finlayson mentioned that every type of fish of the Northern seas could be found in the waters of the Coast of Lewis.

When Finlayson moved to the Lochs area, there was no post office, no roads of any description. The parish church was situated on a small peninsula. It was a new building and seated 700 people. It was the only place of worship in the Lochs area. Since Carloway was a part of the parish, Finlayson would preach in Carloway every three months. At that time the population of Carloway was 901. On Finlayson's arrival as Minister, he found a parish where only 12 people could write. About half of the total population of the parish between the ages of 12 and 24 could read the Gaelic language. The common food for the people were potatoes, bear meal bannocks, pottage made from black oatmeal, milk and fish.

It was to this area that Robert Finlayson came in 1831. When he arrived, the population of the Lochs area was 3300. At the last communion before he became Minister, there had only been 23 communicants. One of the great hindrances Finlayson found was the total lack of roads. He made his way from village to village, catechizing, teaching people the Word of God. Lochs was a moral wilderness. The people had lived in this neglected area for so long that they sat in darkness. Suddenly, the breath of heaven began to blow across this isolated area of Lewis. Suddenly, the old order began to change and something new started happening. Finlayson's ministry was characterized by his pastoral oversight, faithful, expository preaching, catechizing. The whole parish became so transformed that it was like a fresh wind from heaven had blown across the land.

In these years of 1840-43, a new tide of great spiritual life rolled over the whole Isle of Lewis. The solid preaching of the Word of God had broken down many pagan superstitions and beliefs that had held the people in bondage for generations. The people of Lewis had long believed in witches, fairies, and ghosts. One day, Dr. Charles Macrae, a son of the Barvas minister, asked a Lochs boy who herded sheep if there were still any fairies at Lochs. The boy replied, "No! They all left when Mr. Finlayson came." (6)

The ministry of Robert Finlayson could be summed up in his first sermon when he became minister at Knock. He preached from the text, "Behold, the Lamb of God." His passion was Jesus Christ. The only word he knew to give was Jesus Christ. The church was packed on Sundays, and people came to the manse for family worship during the week. Soon, the manse was crowded with people, upstairs and downstairs on week day evenings. Some men and women spoke of these evening meetings at the manse as "sitting at Heaven's gate." (7)

It became quite the popular thing to do in the parish of Lochs for the people to memorize the sayings of Robert Finlayson. He spoke with such conviction, quaint sayings, and sometimes humor that what he said was easily remembered. When he arrived in Lochs in 1831, he asked one of the church office-bearers if he was given to prayer. The man replied that he was, and then asked, "Would you like to hear me pray?" Finlayson said that he would. The man began praying. He started by reciting the Lord's Prayer, then added many words of his own, then finished with the Lord's Prayer. When he finished praying, he asked Finlayson what he thought of his prayer. Finlayson replied, "Well, it had a beautiful beginning, and ended equally as well, but in between were wood, hay and stubble." (8)

Some of Finlayson's sayings which have passed down through the years are as follows:

He was once preaching in the school in the village of Balallan. He said, "O Balallan, you are the devil's kitchen where he cooks his meals. He may dine elsewhere, at Keose, or Cromore or Crossbost, but it is here he cooks. O Balallan, throw water on those cooking fires." (9)

Finlayson was once sailing on a boat when he sighted a school of porpoises. He cried out, "O poor porpoises, what will you do when there shall be no more sea?"

On one occasion, when Finlayson was preaching on Jonah, he said, "Look at that whale. It was in a terrible way. It amazed all the whales. It flung about outrageously, and made a terrific stir. O whale, what is wrong with you?' was shouted at it from the throats of the vastly deep. What is wrong with me? I'm all wrong together. Pains are shooting all through me. I have a prophet of God inside of me, and he is praying, and I can tell you I never wish to taste one again. Praying prophets are no food for whales.' Throw him up, then, if you are in sore trouble'. I wish I could, but I can't.' And the poor whale left its school, and plunged desperately, shooting into every shoal of fish, and creating consternation. At last, after a day of intense anguish, the disgorging moment arrived, and the big fish threw Jonah out of its mouth with such force that he landed on the dry earth." (10)

When the Great Disruption of 1843 occurred, Finlayson and the Lochs Church joined the Free Church movement. He moved the congregation to Crossbost. When revival came to the Lochs area in 1840-43, it brought about the establishment of prayer meetings in Balallan, Laxay, Leurbost, Ranish, Gravir, and Loch Shell. The whole area flourished with the breath of the Holy Spirit.

Robert Finlayson lived very close to heaven. When the congregation moved from Keose to Crossbost in 1843, and became a Free Church, there was a small cave near by the manse. Into this cave Robert Finlayson would go and spend hours and hours in prayer. He had a living passion to tell men and women of a Christ who could and would save them. Quite often, as he preached, he would lean over the pulpit and, with tears streaming down his face, he would plead with the unsaved to come to Christ.

Finlayson served the Lochs and Crossbost Church for 25 years. Finally he moved to the Free Church in Helmsdale in 1856. His last sermon was on, "The Marriage Supper of the Lamb". He died in 1861, at the age of 69.

The Revival of 1840-43 on the Isle of Lewis affected the feelings of the people across the whole island. This revival was so closely akin to the Revival of 1824-28, that sometimes it is difficult to distinguish between the two.

I believe it would also be correct to say that the events leading up to the Great Disruption of 1843 helped to germinate the seeds of revival. As the ministers and the people began to think about the hardships and trials of separation from the established church, there came into the hearts of the people a deep, abiding longing for God. This culminated in great revival.

There were several fruits which began to grow on the tree of revival on the Isle of Lewis. One of the first fruits of the revival was that it put a stop to Sabbath desecration. The people began to remember the Sabbath Day and to keep it holy.

Another fruit of the revival was the deep affection and attachment of the people to their evangelical ministers.

Another fruit was the instituting of family worship in the home. All homes, even those of unbelievers, had family devotions. If the father of a home was away, the mother would conduct family worship. Fishermen who were at sea would hold worship on their boats.

Another fruit of this revival was the fact that catechizing became a regular and deeply appreciated event. Adults permitted themselves to be catechized as well as their children. The local minister would examine every individual in his parish once a year. This not only instilled a great amount of biblical knowledge into the heart and mind of each individual, but it also gave the minister an intimate knowledge of his people.

Rev. Robert Finlayson

Chapter four

"THE REVIVAL OF 1857-1860"

('DUSGADH 1857-1860)

Of all the revivals throughout church history, perhaps none has been more widespread, far-reaching, and powerful than the Revival of 1857-60. So many countries came under its spell. So many people were added to the Kingdom of God. So many churches felt the divine breath of the Holy Spirit.

It is difficult, if not impossible, to ever name a beginning place of revival. It is best to simply say that revival has its beginning in the mind and purpose of God. However, humanly speaking, the Revival of 1857-60 had its beginning in America. On September 23, 1857, Jeremiah Lanphier began a midday prayer meeting on Fulton Street in New York City. By October, this had grown into a daily prayer meeting attended by hundreds of businessmen. By March, 1858, newspapers were running front page reports of 6,000 people attending daily prayer meetings in New York and Pittsburgh, and daily prayer meetings were being held in Washington in five different locations to accommodate the crowds. These prayer meetings began to spread across the nation. In the city of Denver, Colorado and Portland, Oregon, downtown businesses started closing for two hours in the middle of the day so employees could attend prayer meetings. By May, 1859,50,000 people in New York City, out of a total population of 800,000 had been converted to Jesus Christ. New England was totally changed by this revival. In several towns no unconverted adults could be found in the entire town. It was during this revival of 1857-60 that the blind composer, Fannie Crosby, came to faith in Jesus Christ. It was during this revival that a Christian layman made his way to the back of a shoe store and led a teen-age boy to Christ. The boy's name was Dwight L. Moody. Many of our dearest and most cherished hymns came out of this great revival in America; "There shall be showers of blessings", "My Jesus, I love thee", and "What a Friend we have in Jesus". It is estimated that over 1 million people were converted to Christ in America during the Revival of 1857-60.

The Revival of 1857-60 is the most meaningful revival in all of church history to me. The reason: I am who I am today, a saved man, because of the Revival of 1857-60. In 1858, my Great-great Grandfather, Abijah Allen, bought a farm north of Winnsboro, Louisiana. He and my Great-great Grandmother, Mary, had two children. A Baptist preacher came into the area to preach a Aprotracted meeting" in a farmhouse. Abijah and Mary Allen rode horseback to the meeting. The crowds were so great that people filled the farmhouse, and the front porch. The preacher stood in the front door of the house, and preached "both ways." My Great-great Grandparents were converted to Christ, and, within a year Abijah Allen was called to preach. He preached less than two years when he went off to the Civil War, and never returned home, dying in Charlottesville, Virginia.

Because the Spirit of God was moving across America, my ancestors found peace with God through our Lord Jesus Christ, and that same Spirit has found a lodging place in my own heart.

In September, 1857, the same month the prayer meetings began in New York City, four young Irishmen started a prayer meeting in Kells, Ireland. This was the beginning of the Ulster Revival of 1859 in which 100,000 converts to Jesus Christ were added to the churches of Ireland.

The revival then spread to Wales. The story of what happened in that little country is penetrating and glorious. One-tenth of the total population of Wales was converted to Christ.

Charles Haddon Spurgeon, the Pastor of the

Metropolitan Tabernacle in London, England said of these times, "The times of refreshing from the presence of the Lord have at last dawned upon our land. A spirit of prayer is visiting our churches. The first breath of the rushing mighty wind is already discerned, while on rising evangelists the tongues of fire have evidently descended." (1)

Word of revival in America, Ireland, and Wales reached the churches of Scotland and the Hebrides Islands. A deep hunger began to churn in the spirits of ministers and people alike. Suddenly and wonderfully the Spirit of God broke through in Scotland. Revival came on a massive scale. In Scotland 300,000 people were converted to Christ, out of a total population of 3 million.

The Isle of Lewis became a partaker of the Revival of 1857-60. Whereas some of the revivals on Lewis were localized in different parishes, the Revival of 1857-60 impacted the entire island. God became very real. Churches were brought to a sense of renewal. Many people were converted to Christ. Some of the church ministers who knew revival from earlier years were now older, and looking forward to another visitation from God. Some younger ministers had never seen God move in great revival, and were eager to witness the raining down of the Holy Spirit on their parishes

In 1859, the Spirit of God fell in all of His glory on the Isle of Lewis. By the next year, 1860, the Moderator of the Free Church of Scotland, while addressing the General Assembly stated, "We, as a church, accept the revival as a great and blessed fact. Numerous and explicit testimonies from ministers and members alike bespeak the gracious influence upon the people." (2)

In May, 1960, as Dr. Buchanan was closing the Free Church Assembly, he made this statement, "From East

Lothian to the Outer Hebrides, from the shore of the Moray Firth to those of the Solway, and all through the central mining and manufacturing districts of the Kingdom, we heard of scenes which carried us back to the days of the Lord at Shotts and Stewartson and Cambuslang. Unless we greatly deceive ourselves, no former revival of religion which our Church and country have witnessed has ever spread over so wide a field." (3)

The southern end of the Isle of Lewis is known as Harris. Rev. John Macleod gave a report concerning the school in Marig. He said, "Some of the children were deeply affected, and impressed with a sense of their sins, whilst reading their lessons. Parents who were careless about their souls are now seeking their way to Zion, attending regularly on the means of grace, and thirsting for the water of life." (4) A Gaelic school teacher at Steinish on the Isle of Lewis gave this report in November, 1859, "I commenced an evening class for adults about the beginning of November, but owing to the awakening in this place and the people attending sermons or prayer meetings every night in the week (except Saturday), I was obliged to discontinue it. (5)

Perhaps the most influential instrument of God in the Revival of 1857-60 on the Isle of Lewis was a man named Peter Maclean. He became known as the "Lion of the Lews." Peter was born in Uig in 1800. He became a merchant in his own native village. When Rev. Alexander Macleod came to Uig in 1824, his preaching plunged Peter Maclean into deep conviction. He closed up his little store and made his way out to the hills where he spent an entire week seeking God. At midnight, all alone in the hills, Peter Maclean came to faith in Jesus Christ. He rushed back to his village, woke up the people of the village and called them out for a praise service.

As a thank-offering to God for saving him, Peter Maclean canceled all the debts which his customers owed him.

Soon after his conversion, Peter Maclean wrote out a Covenant with God. The Covenant read, "I hereby earnestly purpose in the strength and grace of God, before the Father, the Son and the Holy Ghost, before God's angels in Heaven, the saints on earth, the wicked of the world and the devils in Hell, to dedicate my soul, my body, and my talents to the Lord and His service for time and for eternity, and oh that the Lord, whom I serve, would grant me grace to fulfill this as long as I live, and to Him be glory for ever and ever. To this I now put my hand for my Lord". (6)

Peter was invited to come to Cape Breton, Nova Scotia. This invitation appealed to him. He accepted the call to Cape Breton because he was convinced it was his duty to go. He was ordained in Cape Breton in 1837, and a deep movement of revival began in Cape Breton. He returned to Lewis in 1842, then went as Minister of the Free Church on the Island of Mull. In 1853 he was sent by the General Assembly as its deputy to Cape Breton. The people crowded the building every time he preached. Finally, in 1855, Peter Maclean came to the Free Church of Stornoway on the Isle of Lewis as Minister. Maclean walked the streets of Stornoway perfectly dressed, with a high collar, white stockings, shining cuffs, and a tall, black silk hat.

When the Revival of 1857-60 crossed from Ireland to Scotland, Peter Maclean welcomed it with open arms. He was preaching a Communion Service at Garrabost when, suddenly, the Wind of Pentecost began to blow through the congregation. Maclean gloried in revival. What joy was his as he saw revival sweep over the entire island. Maclean threw himself into the revival body and soul. He preached with an anointing from heaven. He moved among the people day and night. Finally his labors among the people, long tedious hours in the work of the Lord took their toll. His health broke, and for two years he was laid aside. He finally returned to the pulpit, preaching three times every Sabbath Day in the old Free Church on Kenneth Street in Stornoway. His preaching stayed true to his calling. With tears falling down his face, he would give a picture of Christ pursuing the sinner in yearning, deep mercy, and of the poor bewitched sinner fleeing wildly from the Savior.

He preached a Communion Service in his native Uig, and traveled home in the rain. This trip brought on a severe bout with bronchitis and a horrible cough. For 15 months he was ill and for 9 of those months he was confined to his bed. On March 28, 1868, Peter Maclean passed into glory.

This was a man who knew the Wind of the Spirit of God. He gloried in revival, and came to see it change his life, the life of his church, and the life of his home, the Isle of Lewis.

Across all the years of revival on the Isle of Lewis, there have been remarkable women of prayer, women who knew how to get in touch with God at the throne of mercy. During the Revival of 1857-60, one of those ladies was Catherine Mackay of Barvas. Catherine once said, "If I were told that only two out of this generation were to go to heaven, I should hope to be one; and if I were told that only two were to be lost, I should fear to be one of these." (7) It was Catherine Mackay who had such a deep spiritual kinship with John Mackay of Barvas. She once voiced a wish that if the Lord had decreed to shut her out of heaven she might be allowed the favor of a little window through which she could look up at John Mackay in his happiness. John Mackay went to Canada at a relatively young age. On the day he died, Catherine at once knew it, although there had been no communication between them throughout the years of separation.

In the years of revival in 1857-60, Catherine held to the promises of God. She would approach the Lord with every need, every need she had and every need the people had. She prayed with full confidence that God would fulfill His promises. It is to women like Catherine Mackay that we owe so much.

Another person who was instrumental in the Revival of 1857-60 on the Isle of Lewis was John Macrae. In the Hebrides Islands and the Highlands of Scotland, he became known as Macrath Mor (Big Macrae). He gained this nickname because of his size and strength.

Macrae was born in 1794 in Kintail, the son of a farmer. He was herding sheep when he allowed the sheep to move close to the area where Macdonald of Ferintosh, "The Apostle of the North" was preaching. The throb of conviction entered his heart. Macrae made his way to Communion services at Ferintosh. He heard a sermon preached by Dr. "ngus Mackintosh, and the peace of Jesus Christ entered his heart.

Macrae taught school in Uig under the supervision of Rev. Alexander Macleod. Macrae was present and active during the great revival of 1824-28 in Uig. He was ordained at Cross, Ness in 1833. In 1839 he went to a church in Knockbain. At Knockbain he became close friends with Stewart of Cromarty. When Stewart died, Macrae wept like a child. Macrae felt he could no longer stay at Knockbain. In 1849 he was called to the Gaelic Free Church in Greenock, Scotland. In 1857, Macrae came full circle by moving back to the Isle of Lewis. He accepted the church at Lochs. The Revival of 1857-60 , which had its beginning in Knock, began to sweep across the island. We need to remember that Big

Macrae was no stranger to revival. He had seen it, been involved in it in the village of Uig from 1824-28. When the Revival of 1857-60 moved from America and crossed the Atlantic to Ireland, on a Sabbath morning, Big Macrae preached from Psalm 68:18, "Thou hast ascended on high. Thou hast led captivity captive; Thou hast received gifts for men; yea, for the rebellious also, that the Lord God might dwell among them." Big Macrae entitled this sermon, "Gifts for Men." In the sermon, Macrae said, "Perhaps the Holy Ghost is crossing the Irish Channel at this moment. God grant we may feel His power." (8)

That prayer of Macrae's was almost immediately answered. Lochs found itself in the middle of a great, wonderful spiritual awakening. Suddenly the number of people attending church became so great that the worship services had to be moved outside, because the church building was unable to hold the huge crowds. A great spirit of repentance swept over the church members. Unbelievers began to throw themselves on the mercy of Jesus Christ.

At the height of the revival in Lochs, severe desolation visited John Macrae. His beloved wife, Penelope, died. A combination of age, the death of his wife, and the increasing demands of a large church field finally wore Macrae down. In 1866, he accepted a call from the congregation of the church at Carloway. The revival that had swept across the parish of Lochs had also moved across the parish of Carloway. He labored in a wonderful way in Carloway, but health and age required him to submit his resignation in 1871. He moved to Stornoway where he frequently preached at the Free Church of Stornoway. Peter Maclean, the Minister of the Free Church in Stornoway, had died in 1868. Toward the end of his life, a double blessing came. John Macrae (Macrath Mor) knew a year of preaching in Stornoway as people were being saved, and it became a memorable year for the church to have the incomparable Macrath Mor in their pulpit. It was the greatest year of glory the Stornoway church had ever known. Every Sunday Macrath Mor lifted the congregation to the gates of heaven.

Macrae finally moved back to Greenock. While leaning against a parapet one day, he told a friend, "I am now like an old almanac, out of date." (9) John Macrae died on October 9, 1876.

Rev. Peter Maclean

Chapter five

"THE REVIVAL OF 1900-1903"

('DUSGADH 1900-1903)

Revival came once again to the Isle of Lewis from 1900-03. However, this revival came amidst upheaval, division, and torn relationships. The upheaval occurred because of the merger of the United Presbyterian Church and the Free Church in 1900.

It is a bit difficult to keep up with the string of church divisions and mergers in Scotland through the years, but to put it as simply as possible:

In 1733 the Secession Church was formed by withdrawing from the Church of Scotland. In 1761 the Relief Church was formed by withdrawing from the Church of Scotland. In 1843 the Great Disruption occurred, resulting in the formation of the Free Church. In 1847 the United Presbyterian Church was formed in a split from the Church of Scotland.

The upheaval that occurred in 1900 happened when the Free Church and the United Presbyterian Church merged, and became the United Free Church of Scotland. The vast majority of the Free Church members went with the merger, but a small minority chose to remain as members of the Free Church.

When this merger became official, church members were divided, family members were divided, and workers in the field and in the fishing boats were divided. Both denominations; the United Free and the Free Church laid claim to the buildings and property of individual churches. The Free Church from which the majority had departed claimed to be the real Free Church, and claimed all of the property of the Free Church. The Court of Session disallowed the claim, but the Free Church was successful on an appeal to the House of Lords. Finally the British Parliament intervened and made a division of the properties. For instance, in the village of Uig, the property was given to the United Free Church.

When the dust finally settled over the merger of the Free Church and the United Presbyterian Church, the remnant that wanted to remain as the Free Church of Scotland was almost left in a state of destitution. They only had a handful of ministers left, very few houses of worship, no college, and no professors to train young men for the ministry.

It was into this situation that Almighty God suddenly stepped in great revival. It is just like God to come in all of His glory and do a work where it seemed nothing could be done. When people were estranged from one another, when church members were angry with one another, when some churches were locked from the inside to keep ministers and members from entering, this was a wonderful time for God to come in spiritual awakening.

Norman Macleod said that as far as he could discover, the revival of 1900-03 began on the Island of Bernera. (1). Bernera is a tiny, tiny little island off the coast from the village of Uig. Bernera was a part of the parish of Uig, and maybe had a population of 300-400 people. The revival on Bernera had its beginning under the preaching of Rev. Donald Macarthur of Uig who was the Interim-Moderator of the United Free Church of Bernera. The movement spread across the whole island. At that time, the United Free Church and the Free Church were both without ministers, and there developed a strong fellowship between the two congregations, as they worked together for the Lord.

In the Parish of Carloway, the dissension became so great over the merger that some men were threatening to manhandle any who attempted to take possession of the church. Two men, Donald Macarthur and Norman Macarthur actually locked themselves in the church all night, believing that possession was nine/tenths of the law. In Carloway, a great spiritual awakening began in 1903 and spread throughout the village, and then on to the villages of Cross and Lochs.

The Revival of 1900-03 began to spread across Lewis. It moved to Bravas, and on to Ness. Rev. Mackay said, "A large number of old and young have been convicted of sin by the Spirit of God, and turned from darkness to light, finding peace and joy in believing. The people have come out to church in a very marked way for miles every day. Indeed, all manual labor was for a time given up, and the worshipers returned home at night singing the praises of God." (2) Rev. Peter Macdonald of Stornoway spoke of the revival as one of the deepest spiritual movements that had ever been known in the island.

When the revival moved to the northern end of the Isle of Lewis to the village of Ness, it brought times of wonderful blessings and deep searching. "During the Communion services, held amid much discomfort, it was felt that there was something unusual about the services. Those who spoke felt as if they had unusual liberty; those who listened that it was a time of blessing. On the Sabbath evening some of the Lord's people who stayed for a prayer meeting melted down, and many said that the Lord was in that place. On Monday there was a deep solemnity about the service, and the minister felt the interest to be so deep that he followed up the services with a series of meetings. At the second of those, strong men had to leave the meeting, crying out, What must I do to be saved?'" (3) These meetings at Ness continued for six weeks, night after night, and many people were saved.

The revival came to the village of Tolsta Chaolais, near Carloway. Norman Macdonald visited the village at the peak of the revival. He went into a home where a large number of new converts had gathered. He noticed they were expressing their Christian joy with much laughter, and he felt uneasy about them doing this. He felt so uneasy about it that he went outside to pray. When he entered the yard, the Spirit of God spoke to him and said, "These are not drunken as ye suppose, seeing it is but the third hour of the day." Norman Macdonald returned back into the house. He entered into the joy of the new converts, and suddenly collapsed into a swoon.(4)

I have always been intrigued by women of great faith during times of revival. During the times of revival on the Isle of Lewis, it was unknown numbers of women who paid the price in intercessory prayer, and deep devotion to Jesus Christ. It seemed to be the women who lived life somewhere between heaven and earth.

During the Revival of 1900-03, one of the impressive women of Lewis was Margaret Maciver of Ness. Margaret began to seek after the Lord when she was twelve years of age. When she was still a young lady, she had a dream in which she saw the resurrection morning. She saw herself rising out of the grave to welcome the Redeemer. This dream was so real and vivid to her that she retained each detail of it for the rest of her life.

Several years after this dream, Margaret married a man named Mackenzie. She and her new husband made their home in North Tolsta. As she looked around at her new home, she recognized the scene as the exact place she had seen in her dream years before. More than seventy years later, Margaret was buried in that very spot.

Margaret had an unusual gift to impart words of wisdom to young Christians. She was once talking to a young Christian and said, "Ask the Lord to enable you to pray in the

Spirit. Only in prayer do we enjoy true nearness to Him and taste of His love. Hide nothing from Him, and the more He shows you of your sins and sinfulness the more you will thank Him. Whatever you do, take Him always at His Word." (5)

Margaret lived her life enjoying the secrets of God. She had a Word from God while seriously ill that God would raise her up. When her last grandchild was born, she said, "This tells me that my prolonged life is coming to an end, for He promised me, peace, when I should see my children's children." (6)

Two weeks before Margaret died, a friend found her weeping. Margaret said, "Today my thoughts are down in the place where my bones shall lie till the last trump shall sound. My soul is already in eternity, and the only obstacle between me and the full enjoyment of God is this frail body." (7) Fourteen days later, in June, 1940, Margaret went to glory.

In the Revival of 1949-53 that came to the Isle of Lewis, a young lady by the name of Mary Morrison was converted to Christ. Mary went on to a life of service to the Lord with the Faith Mission. She later married a man from South Africa named Colin Peckham. For many years Dr. Peckham was Principal of the Faith Mission College. In February, 2004, it was a privilege to have Dr. Peckham and Mary in our home for lunch. During the lunch, Mary told me a story about the Revival of 1900-03 that touched my heart in a deep way.

Mary grew up in the northern end of the Isle of Lewis in Ness. She said during the Revival of 1900-03 her Grandfather, Murdo Macfarlane, walked from Ness to Uig for Communion Services. This is a distance of over thirty miles. Mr. Macfarlane walked bare foot, carrying his shoes in his hands so he would not wear them out. When he arrived at the church in Uig, young girls were waiting with water and towels, washing the feet of the saints of God as they arrived. What a blessed story I found that to be!

Some wonderful effects came from the Revival of 1900-03. These effects made a distinct difference in the lives of the people of Lewis for many years.

1. The upheaval of the merger of the United Presbyterian Church and the Free Church caused the people to study much more closely particular doctrines of the church, so that they were well grounded in the Word of God.

2. Those who heard the Word of God preached found that the deep feelings of their own heart were being spoken of by the ministers.

3. Family worship was begun in many homes where it had been neglected for a long time.

4. Communion Season became very precious to the people.

5. A great, deep burden for the lost people of the community came to the hearts of the believers.

6. The way of life that the people had known became quite tasteless to them. They forsook amusements that many people today would regard as harmless.

Chapter six

"THE REVIVAL OF 1923-1926"

('DUSGADH 1923-1926)

The Revival of 1923-26 on the Isle of Lewis was more localized than other revival movements. Whereas other great revivals poured forth over the entire island, in 1923-26, revival seemed to be confined to two parishes; Ness and Carloway.

It is always amazing how we human beings can so easily forget the blessings of God. God can come, in all of His glory, on a church, and in the matter of a few short years that church can move past the spirit of revival to a spirit of complacency and deadness. That is exactly what happened in the Bible. God would pour forth on His people, but they would then turn their backs upon Him, and revival was needed again.

The spirit of revival that came to the parish of Carloway during this time, one might not call true revival. It was most assuredly a time of the showers of blessings, but it did not compare with the great deluge of revival that was to come to Carloway in another decade.

In 1924, Rev. John Maciver was ordained and installed as the minister of the church in Carloway. Mr. Maciver had been through personal struggles of his own. He had thoughts of leaving the ministry. When he was asked to visit a man who was very ill, he prayed that the man would find rest and peace that night. He also told the Lord he would take it as a sign from God to stay in the ministry if the man did find rest and peace.

Sometime later Mr. Maciver saw the man, and asked about his health. The man told Mr. Maciver that a miracle had happened the night Maciver prayer for him. The man said, "I not only slept well, but I knew also why you had prayed." (1)

The Carloway church had known some years of deadness. The years of 1923-26 under the leadership of Mr. Maciver began to bring life to the church. Bones begin to come together, but flesh would not appear on them, nor would they stand up to full life for another decade when the glory of God suddenly burst on the scene. Maciver had an unusual anointing in his preaching. He often would leave his audience in tears as he spoke of the sufferings of the Redeemer.

In the village of Ness, the church had been for some time in a spirit of apathy. In 1923 Rev. Roderick J. Macleod was installed as minister of the Free Church in Ness, and without any preparation, with no advance warning, the Spirit of God began to move in the lives of both congregations of Ness. For some time few, if any, young people had been attending church in Ness, but when the Revival of 1923-26 came, young people began to seek the Lord. Many young people were saved. The Spirit of God fell on people of all ages, but one unique feature of this revival: more men were affected by the revival than women.

Rev. Murdoch Campbell, in speaking of this revival and Roderick Macleod, said, "He had hardly commenced his work there than signs began to multiply that God's Spirit was at work through his earnest and Scriptural preaching. A large number were brought out of darkness into light, and to the end of their days the lives and witness of those men and women showed that they were wrought in God." (2)

Rev. Donald Macdonald was one of the young people who was saved during this time of revival. He said, "When I was a young Christian, it was during a time of revival under the ministry of the late Rev. Roderick John Macleod, there were lots of young people converted in that revival, and we were as happy as the days were long. The sun of God's favor was shining on our tabernacle and we were full of the joy of the Lord." (3)

The revival stopped in 1926 when Roderick Macleod

moved to the church in Dumbarton. Rev. Roderick Macleod died at the age of 37.

Chapter seven

“THE REVIVAL OF 1934-1939”

(‘DUSGADH 1934-1939)

From 1949-53 there was a great, wonderful revival that swept over the Isle of Lewis. The principal preacher during this revival was the Scottish Highlander preacher, Duncan Campbell. Across the years, this revival has received more publicity, and more has been written about it than any other revival movement on Lewis. However, the Revival of 1934-39 has been called by many the most powerful, most intense revival to ever grace the shores of the Isle of Lewis.

The Revival of 1934-39 had its beginning in the Church at Carloway, then it spread to other parishes; Bernera, Park, Kinloch, Lochs, Knock, Bravas, and Cross. Before the revival began, the church membership of the Free Church in Carloway was made up of middle-aged and elderly people. There was only one person under forty years of age who was a communicant. The young people of the parish had given themselves wholly to worldly amusements. Their lives were caught up in football, concerts, dances, and the ceilidh (kay-lee). The ceilidh was a gathering in a house where there was music, dancing, story-telling, and drinking. Before the revival, the ceilidh was held on the Sabbath as well as on week-nights.

Rev. John Maciver had been inducted as Minister of the Church in Carloway in 1924. For the first ten years of his ministry, he preached fervently on the sufferings of Jesus Christ. He prayed in an agonizing way for revival, but with little to show. A few times he was deeply tempted to accept calls from other churches, but could not bring himself to leave Carloway. During these first ten years, Rev. Maciver saw a few showers of blessing, but no great outpouring of the Holy Spirit.

Then, in the spring of 1934, Rev. Malcolm Maciver of Crossbost, who was a prayer partner of Rev. Maciver for revival, had a dream. He dreamed that he and John Maciver were sitting in the church at Carloway, listening to another preacher. When the preacher announced his text, John Maciver turned to Malcolm Maciver and said, "That's the seventh time I have heard him on that text." Malcolm Maciver concluded that since the number seven was the perfect number, and the dream was an indication that revival was at hand, Malcolm left immediately to tell John Maciver. (1)

During that year of 1934, John Maciver began to feel an unusual freedom and liberty in his preaching. A number of young men began to attend prayer meetings, and the attendance at both the Free Church and the Church of Scotland began to show a marked increase. It was quite evident in the services that the Spirit of God was beginning to move.

The Revival of 1934-39 did see prostrations (people falling under the power of God), and other physical manifestations. Most of the physical manifestations were seen in Shader and Barvas, where the raising of hands and praying aloud, almost shouting, had become the custom...When the revival ended the prostrations ended. (2)

The revival continued in full strength across the island through 1939, but by 1940 the revival had subsided, and the churches returned to normal. Many have thought that one of the main reasons the revival movement abated was because of the large number of young men and women who went off to World War II. When these Lewis men and women returned from the war, the revival was gone.

But, during the years of the revival, churches became crowded, the multitudes at Communion Seasons were enormous. "Churches were full, and the solemnity at those services was awe-inspiring as the Word of God went as fiery darts to the consciences and hearts of the unconverted....the subject of conversation was the work of the Lord in our district and those who had been converted. Bha n aite air ghoil', (The place was agog). A (3)

The effect on the people was astounding. There came a deep conviction of sin, an abiding concern for their eternal welfare, a sense of unworthiness, agonizing prayer for mercy, a thirst for more knowledge of the Bible. Some of the people felt as if they were, "groping in the dark to find true peace in Christ, and were in this state for a considerable time." (4)

One of the most remarkable elements of this revival was its deep impact on the young. They began to show a deep hatred of sin. They immediately abandoned their former life-style. The young converts dreaded to have any blemish in their life that would bring shame on Jesus Christ.

The revival did not touch the very young, although some converts were in their mid-teens. Neither did the revival appear to touch many of the hard and aged people. (5)

One of the unique elements of this revival was the beginning of "house meetings." These meetings were for the young converts of the revival. There were prayers, worship and discussion. It is interesting that no office-bearers of the church, nor none of the more advanced believers were allowed to attend these meetings. No members of the opposite sex were permitted. Young converts would simply meet, pray, worship the Lord, and discuss their conversion. They usually went home full of joy, and their hearts stirred by the Holy Spirit.

I want to share with you the stories of five of the most interesting, powerful, colorful men who came out of the Carloway Revival. These five men were; Murdo Macleod, John Macleod, Duncan Macphail, Murdo Macaulay, and Roddy Mackay.

MURDO MACLEOD

Murdo Macleod was called, "Murdigan." He grew up in Kirivick, a village close by Carloway. His father, Iain Ruadh, was an elder in the Church of Scotland. Murdigan had no interest in religion. He seemed to live in a dark world of no spirituality at all. He never entered a church door, had no use for any Christian beliefs. Especially, he had no use for the doctrines of the Incarnation and the Resurrection of Jesus Christ. People talked about Murdigan, that they saw no hope of him ever being converted to Christ. The people who knew him said that he was beyond redemption.

One young lady, Catriona Alasdair regarded Murdigan as an out- and- out enemy of the truth. (6) One night, a group of young converts had gathered for one of the "house meetings" when Murdigan walked in. The young converts were discussing the resurrection of Jesus. Murdigan shouted, "Surely you do not believe that nonsense?" Everyone was silent, for the young converts were all quite afraid of him. They got up and walked out, moved to another house. Murdigan followed them. Catriona Alasdair remarked, "Why is that devil following the poor boys?" No one was aware at this time that the Spirit of God was already working in Murdigan's heart.

The first workings of the Holy Spirit in Murdigan's life happened in March, 1936. At the Communion Season, he decided to go to church. He did not walk with the crowd, didn't want to be seen going to church. He wanted to get there late, and get a seat at the back, and sit unnoticed by the church crowd. When Murdigan walked in, he saw a seat at the back, a red-cushioned seat, and sat down. He was unaware this was the manse (parsonage) seat and that the minister's wife, Mrs.

Maclennan, had not arrived.

The preacher that evening was Rev. Lachlan Macleod. Something the preacher said that night shook Murdigan to the core. He felt a power coming into him, but he did not darken the door of any church for another three months. That night he was attending the Church of Scotland, but never entered the Church of Scotland again.

For three months Murdigan mulled over and over in his mind what he had heard. One night, lying in bed, he was thinking about all of this, when, suddenly, there appeared before him a vision of the glorified Christ. He was sure that he had seen the Lord with his own eyes. This was an experience that never left Murdigan. For the rest of his life, whenever the minister, or anyone else would quote John 1:14, "and we beheld His glory, the glory as of the only begotten of the Father full of grace and truth", Murdigan would burst out in loud sobs and tears, or else he would break out in a loud giggle. (7)

Through the years, when Murdigan was called on to pray, if he quoted his famous text of John 1:14, he would either give out a long, deep, sigh followed by sobbing, or he would begin giggling, and that would be the end of his prayer. One of his friends asked Murdigan, "Murdigan, when are you going to complete your numerous unfinished prayers?" Murdigan would reply in a hilarious manner, "Ho! Ho! Ho!."

On one occasion at a Communion Season in Ness, a group was gathered in a house for prayer. Murdigan was offering a prayer. After a few words, he quoted his famous text, "We beheld His glory...." There was a deep sigh, then silence. Everyone waited and waited for Murdigan to begin praying again. After a long pause, some looked up, Murdigan was gone. They went outside and saw Murdigan walking across a field one-quarter mile away, making his way to the seashore.

On another occasion, Murdigan and his friend, Tom Macleod, went to a Communion at Knock. In one of the meetings, Murdigan again went into fits of crying and giggling during prayer time. When they left the meeting, Tom Macleod said to Murdigan, "You must tell me why at one time you burst into sobbing and then into laughter." Murdigan begin to laugh aloud. Tom said, "If you won't tell me, I will never go anywhere with you again." Murdigan replied, "When I get a clear view of what Christ suffered for me, I burst into tears, and when I , on the other hand, see His great love for me, I go into fits of laughter." (8)

Murdigan had little sympathy for those who were not like him. His vision of Christ as he was lying in bed was so real to him, the glory of Christ was so brilliant that he pulled the sheet over his head to hide his face from him. In later years, Murdigan mellowed in his critical nature of others who were not like him. He had a dream. In the dream he saw a young woman dressed in dark clothes. There appeared a large white house and the girl in black entered the main door. Murdigan also tried to enter, but he felt the door getter smaller and smaller, and he was just able to squeeze through. When he got through, this Scripture came to him, "Jesus said to him, Thomas, because you have seen me, you have believed. Blessed are those who have not seen and yet have believed" (John 20:29).

JOHN MACLEOD

John Macleod, known locally on Lewis as "An Cor", grew up in the village of Garenin. Garenin is a small village of black houses, which are the traditional thatched houses of Lewis. These houses were abandoned in 1973, but have been restored today.

John Macleod joined the large group of people from Lewis who left the island in 1923-24 to emigrant to America and Canada. These two years saw thousands of islanders leave because of the destitution on Lewis. John Macleod was one of these who went to Canada. After he arrived in Canada, Macleod illegally entered America. He was taken into custody and sent back to Lewis in 1932. Macleod said when he left Lewis a Bible was put in his suitcase, and when he returned eight years later it was still unopened.

When he returned home, he followed the usual custom of attending Communion Season which was held at Shawbost. He said, "I went to the Shawbost Communion, mainly to flirt with girls my own age. I went to see a friend, and at bedtime there was no male who could conduct family worship in his house. Murdo (my friend) said he would read a chapter and a psalm, but he would neither sing nor pray....There was an old lady from Lochs in the house, she was then 84 years old. She turned to me and said, Go on your knees and pray.' No', I said, I have no prayer', for I had never prayed in my life.' Finally the old lady prayed herself.....I did not forget her conversation with us." (9)

In 1935, three years after the conversation with the old lady from Lochs, Macleod went to church one evening. He told his friend, sitting beside him, to wake him up when the service was over so he would not be left asleep in the church. Rev. William Campbell of Knock was preaching that night. Macleod said that Campbell was speaking of the crown of thorns on Christ. Suddenly the words drew Macleod's attention, then, the words began to disturb him. When he got home that night, for the first time he began to pray. He didn't know what to say in prayer, but he remembered his father reading, "Pilgrims's Progress", so he began praying words, "O

Lord, from my great guilt deliver my soul." Macleod said, "I remember one night praying, and when I rose off my knees the burden was gone and I felt greatly relieved, so that I could now go and indulge in gambling with the boys as before, for I used to be their leader. However, when I turned to go there, as soon as I saw the light of the house the burden came back again, and I could go no further. I found myself then in the same state as before. I cried unto God, and made my way back home. A woman next door came in, and although she was not a member, she said the Truth spoke to her in the door." (10)

The change in John Macleod's (An Cor's) life was remarkable. The spiritual darkness of his former life vanished. He truly became a new creature in Christ Jesus. On his deathbed, the final words he uttered were, "To be with Christ is far better" (Phil. 1:23).

DUNCAN MACPHAIL

Duncan Macphail died in 1941 at the age of 86. "When he died we may say the revival died with him." (11) When the Revival of 1934-39 came, Macphail was 80 years old. He had been a member of the Carloway Church since 1896, and had been a Deacon since 1914. Before the revival, his Christian life had been normal, steady, but when the revival came, no one seemed to be as much revived as old Duncan Macphail. In his book, *The Burning Bush of Carloway*, Murdo Macaulay put it in a beautiful way, "We have often seen in May a lone sheep leaving the rest and skipping with the lambs, and we noticed that this was due usually to its being in better condition than the rest after a hard winter. So it appeared to be with Duncan." (12)

When the revival came, and new converts were being added to the church, it became an absolute delight for the people to listen to Duncan Macphail pray. He would speak of the glorious work of the Redeemer, and then his thoughts would spread all over the world. He would pray for the black people, the yellow people, the Indians, the people of every color.

The young converts would call for Duncan to go with them to the homes for fellowship meetings. Can you see that? Young converts and a man over 80 years of age walking to some distant home to have fellowship with Jesus Christ. When the young would bring him home late at night, he would ask, "Where are you going to gather tomorrow night?"

When praying, Duncan Macphail would often move into talking personally with characters from the Bible. It seemed as though he was personally acquainted with each one of them. One night, in prayer, he began talking to Peter, "Yes, Peter, they put you into prison, and put two chains on you and they thought that they had you, but they did not know with whom they had to reckon, for persevering prayer was made to God by the church for you. But when the angel smote your side, your chains fell off and your keepers did not know that you had gone. Oh, aren't You watchful over Your people!" (13)

Duncan Macphail used the same method in teaching that he did in prayer. Once, as he was teaching, he suddenly turned on the devil, and began talking to him, "You, taking upon you to tempt the Lord your God. You showed him all the kingdoms of the world and their glory as if he had no knowledge but a little like yourself, and you dared to say, All these will I give you if you will fall down and worship me', You bad rascal, you have little claim on them." Everyone present burst into laughter as they heard this rebuke being given to the adversary." (14)

As stated earlier, Duncan Macphail died in 1941. By the time he passed away the revival had faded away.

MURDO MACAULAY

One of the most popular converts of the 1934-39 revival in Carloway was Murdo Macaulay. He was a carefree young man whose main interest in life was playing football (soccer). He was converted to Christ, was called to service during World War II. During the war he was captured and spent three years as a prisoner of war in Germany. It was during his imprisonment that he felt God calling him to preach. When he returned from the war, he went to school, and became a minister. He served from 1956-1975 as the minister of the Back Free Church. He is the author of two wonderful books; "Aspects of the Religious History of Lewis", and "The Burning Bush of Carloway." Macaulay lived past 90 years of age. Until the end of his life, he still read the Bible in Hebrew, Greek, Gaelic, English, and German.

In the late 1980s, Rev. Murdo Macaulay was invited to the Free Church of Stornoway to enter into a discussion with the Stornoway minister, Rev. Murdo Alex Macleod. They spent an evening in the church discussing revival. I think it would be best, at this time, to just allow Rev. Murdo Macaulay to share with us his thoughts on revival, and to tell some about his life, and his dealings with God.

"Revival means bringing life again by the Spirit of God. Some people believe that long periods of prayer bring revival. In one church the minister had been preaching that sort of doctrine. Revival begins in the church through the preaching of the Word. It is really a combination of the Word of God and the Spirit, because the Word is the Sword of the Spirit. There is no other way of doing it. Sometimes people felt constrained to pray

for sometime, but as far as the various prayer groups that are going on, I am a bit skeptical of it.

The primary duty of the minister is to preach the Word of God. Prayer comes in along with it, but it is not the primary duty. The primary duty is to declare the riches of Christ.

In Carloway, in 1934, there were one or two of the old people who said they were looking for somebody to come, but the people had no inkling at all, unless the minister had. He had refused a call to Ness, but I am not certain he would have refused a call to Stornoway, but Kenneth Macrae came to Stornoway and preached two excellent sermons, and that was that.

When revival came to Carloway, there was no increase in church attendance until the revival came. People were taken by surprise because of certain individuals who were converted. They were surprised at my conversion because I was the leader in the area of all evil that was going on. I wasn't at the beginning of the revival. There were a number who came to Christ before me.

I was not feeling anything at the beginning of the revival. I was playing football. I was captain of the team. I was visiting with Murdo Macleod. He asked me about the revival in Carloway. I said to him, 'Well, this fellow lost his mother and this fellow was this and this fellow was that.' I thought this was the reason some fellows were going to church, but this old man knew I didn't know what I was talking about.

At this time, I wasn't wanting to be converted, wasn't thinking of it at all. I went to church regularly. One minister said, 'You are saying that you will be converted. You won't be converted.' That is what I was saying to myself at the time. I didn't want it, didn't feel any need of it. But, I was ill for about a year. I promised relatives that I would go over to the

Communion at Point. I wasn't looking for conversion or anything. Quite a few of the people of Carloway were going to Communion at Point. I went with them. They were singing all the way there. By the time we got to Point, I was singing with them, and I couldn't turn back. I hadn't gone to the prayer meeting, but I went on Thursday, when I came back to Carloway. The revival had started about two years before I was converted."

At this point in the discussion on revival, the minister of the Free Church in Stornoway, Rev. Murdo Alex Macleod, asked, "There is so much of the presence of the Spirit in revival. Did the people who were not converted feel it?"

Murdo Macaulay replied, *"Quite true! The unconverted feel the atmosphere, but they also feel it when it goes away. They noticed that. I was speaking to one man, he wasn't converted. He would go to the meetings and stay until 7:00 in the morning. Another man in Carloway told me that he noticed when the atmosphere changed, a coldness comes in, an indifference. The Spirit withdraws from the meeting. When the Holy Spirit is present, the emotions are moved, and when things would go flat, the unconverted would notice that.*

We didn't have many instances of people who were converted and did not continue. We had one or two later on. There were more questions about doctrine in Carloway than in other places.

Preaching was the main part, then there would be discussions in a home on what was preached. Mr. Maciver was the Minister of the Church of Scotland in Carloway. He was an idol. People would go listen to Maciver. A lady who was looking after her aged mother went to listen to Maciver and told this lady how wonderful Maciver was that night. The minister of the Free Church knocked on the door, admonishing us about going to hear Maciver. He said, 'I think you are going to the extreme when I'm not there.' We lost an awful lot when we did not go to the meetings.

At the end of the revival in Carloway, a busload went down to the meeting in Shader, where there were people waving their hands in the air and going out for the count. Some took that back to Carloway. As far as I know, no one was converted after that. It came to an end.

Mr. Maciver told me, when he was old that there were two girls flinging their hands and going out for the count. They were carried out, and laid on the ground. Mr. Maciver said it didn't interfere with the service in anyway. He didn't lose his liberty. He wasn't for or against what was happening. He would just let it be.

The revival in Carloway began in 1934, and continued to 1939. When I got out of the war, I noticed as soon as the people got out of church, they made straight for home. A number were thinking of getting married. During the revival people would gather in bunches after church. When I came back from the war, I knew the revival was finished, because of the way people were acting after the service. It was a sign of coldness.

I remember a boy in Carloway, before he was converted and before I was converted. I had a bottle of beer. I gave him half a glass of beer. He started praying. I just looked at him. He said he was going to see this girl. He was saying every word his mother would say at worship. He knew it by heart. It all came out after one half glass of beer. That was all he could stand.

People who have been in a revival tend to pray for another one. They uphold the Spirit of God. They are looking and waiting, to see if they can experience it again. No one can know what revival is until it comes."

At this point, Rev. Murdo Alex Macleod asked, "There are some who say we should be satisfied with the ordinary sense of church life. We shouldn't pray for revival that upsets our way life. Why want more?"

Rev. Macaulay replied, *"What does the Word of God say? What were they doing on the day of Pentecost? They were of one mind, praying, but they had to be dependent on the time of the decree. Christians are always longing for more converts. We always try to bend our will to the will of God, but it is not always easy."*

Kenneth Macrae of Stornoway was against prostrations. It was prevalent in Point and in Lochs, but not in Stornoway. Those who were passing out were not out at all. They would be stretched out on the pew and hear every word being said. They appeared to be unconscious, but they weren't.

The elders didn't accept Roderick Macleod in Ness too well, because he jumped the fences. One of the features of revival, the vast majority of those who accept Christ do so before they are 30. There are less before 40, lesser still before they are 50. If you get over that, you're too late. I remember a man who was converted by the words, 'Too late!' He was over 50.

There were some children who were converted during the revival. It may depend on what you call children. My sister was only 16. A lot of early young people were converted.

Today, most of the young people don't go to church. They stay at home, looking at TV. Most of the young people at Carloway were not members of the church.

At that time, we used to go to the Shawbost Communion. Of course, Shawbost belonged to the parish of Carloway. Everyone went to the Shawbost Communion, not just the saved, everyone.

There were several young people and some children

converted in Ness. Donald Macdonald was only 13. Calum Morrison was converted. He was a young person.

The great difficulty we faced was being called on to pray. I was called on to pray before I was a member of the church. It was a most unusual thing to be called on to pray when I wasn't even a member. It was an elder beside me, in a house prayer meeting, who called on me to pray. A group of us, just males, were gathered in a house just to learn how to pray. We didn't allow older Christians to attend because we were afraid they would take charge. I went to that prayer meeting. I had strung a number of texts together which I could reel off, and I was called on first to pray. So, I did reel them off. When I sat down, this fellow got up and said, 'Who do you think is going to pray after that?' This shows how weak we were, but we were encouraging one another. We were getting practice and learning texts of Scripture.

I did not feel any desire to preach. I'll tell you why! A neighbor lady lived about 100 yards from us. She said I was to be a preacher of the gospel when I was born. I got to know this. Some in our house got to calling me the minister. A lady rebuked me. Instead of encouraging me, it did the opposite. I didn't decide to go into the ministry until I went to Germany. It was in Germany that I succumbed to the call.

My first sermon; I was a student in Edinburgh. Mr. Macleod, the evangelist from Greenock, he was a chaplain for the forces at the time. He and I were married to sisters. He phoned me up, and said, "I have to go away. You take the three services tomorrow." I started to protest, and he hung up. I had one sermon that I had heard Macleod preach on Nicodemus. I knew it by heart, but I had two more I had to preach. I was terrified going into the pulpit. Just as the door of the pulpit closed behind me, all fear left me."

Murdo Macaulay went to World War II, was stationed in France, where he was captured, and held as a prisoner of war in Germany. He was always very reluctant to talk about this period of his life, but at this meeting in the Free Church in Stornoway, while discussing revival, Macaulay related his experiences during the war.

"I am reluctant to tell this because it is so personal, because people might think I am trying to make myself look big. I want to make myself smaller and smaller to the very end.

Three years before the war started, I had a vision of an angel coming to my bed. I never saw such a pure specimen of humanity in my life. The angel asked me, 'Where is Germany?' I saw a map of Europe stretched out, and I pointed to Germany. The angel said, 'Well, I am going there.' Then, he went away.

I told this to the people I mixed with. I didn't understand it until I went to France. I told my troop in France that I would be taken prisoner, but I wouldn't be killed. In six months, I was captured.

The Germans broke through in Northern France. We were moved there. I was showing a boy where to place his gun. He went over the fence, and the gun was broken. The bayonet went through his leg, out the bottom of his foot. I bandaged it up, and sent him back to the field hospital.

We were told to retreat. I hoped I could get away with my men. The German guns were covering everything. Our truck left, and all my stuff was in that truck; my Bible, shaving kit, clothes. We were told to break our revolvers, our rifles, everything that might be of use to the Germans.

I was breaking my compass and my binoculars when a big sergeant came over to me, and said, 'Your boys are on the other side of the road.' I didn't know where they were. We had been separated.

The Germans caught up with us. I was captured, and they began leading us down a road. When we were about 200 yards away, I asked one of the Germans for permission to go back to the truck to get something special. The German guard told me I could go, but he would keep an eye on me. I went back. The only thing I took from the truck was my Gaelic Bible.

In the prisoner of war camp, there were thirty-three languages spoken, and that Gaelic Bible was the only textbook we had. I still have that Gaelic Bible." (15)

Murdo Macaulay lived to preach the gospel of Jesus Christ for many years, serving as a church minister, and writing books that have been read by multitudes.

RODDY MACKAY

Roddy Mackay was a teen-age boy at the time of the revival. The information I have concerning his conversion to Christ is contained in a personal letter to Steve Taylor, a law enforcement office on the Island of Skye. Steve is the author of a wonderful book entitled, *The Skye Revivals.* I think it best to simply let Roddy Mackay tell his own story of what happened to him during the Revival of 1934-39.

"I was born in the little village of Tolsta Chaolais in the district of Carloway. The Revival started at the beginning of 1936. I was just over eighteen years old and my past began to give me some concern. I knew that God's Spirit was striving with me and although I didn't know how to pray and nobody ever heard me pray, I tried to ask God for forgiveness and to have mercy on my soul, to forgive me for all the cursing and swearing and the other sins I had committed when I was keeping the sheep away from the crofts.

By this time it was the spring, April, 1936, and every day we heard of somebody new coming out to the prayer meetings. There was hardly a day passed without hearing of somebody being converted. I was very much troubled in my soul by this time and I believed that the Lord was awakening me and calling me to come out on His side, but I didn't have the courage to come out to the prayer meeting yet, although I had the most strong desire to do so. I remember saying to my mother on the Wednesday morning that I thought I would go to the prayer meeting that night. Well, her answer wasn't very encouraging. She said if I did go, I would have to keep going, so I did not go that night.

My parents were adherents of the Church of Scotland, and I knew little or nothing about the church, but my desire to know more was growing. There were only about half a dozen families belonging to the Church of Scotland in the village, and at that time none of them were showing any signs of interest in the things of the church. There was only the one meeting place in the village and both churches shared it. The Church of Scotland minister had a service there once a month. He was a very good man, his name was the Rev. Murdo Maclennan.

In a way I felt on my own, as there was nobody in the village of my own age with whom I could pal around, but there were a lot in the surrounding villages; Breasclete, Callanish, Garrynahine, and Carloway. The big majority were in the Free Church and they were still coming in and being converted. There were two's and three's from the same family being dealt with by God's Spirit. There were not very many households between Garrynhine and Carloway that the Spirit of the Lord did not touch, and here I was with the deepest desire to be among them, feeling on my own, in one sense, and afraid to take the next step. I was praying to the Lord to show me what to do and to give me the courage I required to come out to the prayer meeting. It didn't matter what church. The Lord answered my prayers there when I could not hold out any longer. I finally plucked up courage to go out to the Free Church prayer meeting on the Wednesday night.

On my way to the prayer meeting that night the devil was trying to make me turn back, telling me what a fool I was and that the Free Church elders at the door would ask me what did I want, and what was I going to say to them. But, that was the devil's devices to try to stop me from coming out on the Lord's side.

When I got to the door, I was welcomed with open arms. We had a house meeting after the prayer meeting, and it was in an old Christian's house, and he did ask me when I went in, "and what are you doing here?" Well, I can tell you, I felt very small. I didn't know what to say, but that I had a strong desire to be there, and they then soon put me at ease. There were two or three old Christians from Doune there, and they were praying for the young fellow who was with them that night. There wasn't any of my own age that night in the house. On my way home that night I felt as if a load had fallen off me, and although I still had many burdens, I felt very glad to have had the courage to be in the prayer meeting. I was at the receiving end at home with criticism from my brothers. They were saying to me that it was because I was hearing of others being converted that I went to the prayer meeting. With that and my own doubts, it did not help. However, the Lord gave me the strength to go on with the desire growing stronger to be found in Christ.

The following Sabbath I got up early and got dressed and took my bike and cycled to Carloway to church, the Church of Scotland. On my way to church that morning, I caught up with other young people with the same feelings and doubts and fears as myself. Words fail me to tell of the joy I experienced that day in church. I didn't know how the minister and his wife got to know, but they spoke to me after the service and told me they had heard I was converted. I didn't know what to say. I felt as if I was walking on air.

For a full year after that I can never explain or find words to tell of the glorious transformation that took place in my life, how wonderfully the Lord was working in Lewis at that time, to be caught up in the Spirit of Revival. I got to know young people and old in the surrounding villages by going to house meetings nearly every night of the week, especially in Breasclete and Callanish. It was the most glorious part of my life. I even thought there was something of the Spirit of Revival in the animals around me. We had ten cows and a few sheep at that time, and also thought it was in the glorious weather. I was seeing God at work in everything. Although we were in house meetings nearly every night, we didn't seem to get tired at all. I remember one night being in a prayer house meeting in Breasclete till six o'clock in the morning without any sleep at all. I started on the croft (farm) work as soon as I got home.

The Lord was working wonders every day and a great change was taking place in many young lives and some very rough characters too. There were very hardened men and women softened by the Lord's Spirit. You could see them with tears streaming down their faces in repentance for their past sins, and some of them felt the presence of the Lord so strong that they were overcome and went into trances. It was glorious to be with them, and feeling a part of it was just beyond words." (16)

The Revival of 1934-39 that began in Carloway then moved north on the Isle of Lewis to the Point area. Rev.

William Campbell was the minister of the Knock Free Church at Point, Lewis. He had a real heart to see revival. In 1935 Campbell decided to have special evangelistic services at his church. He invited other Free Church ministers to preach. He was deeply conscious that awakening was very close. The week of special services closed with no visible results. He announced that there would be another week of meetings, and he would do the preaching. He preached on Ezekiel 37, the valley of dry bones. That night the fire of God fell in great blessing.

In 1936, the revival moved into the villages of Shader, Aignish, Kinloch, Balallan and Barvas. One young convert, Sandy Mor, decided that he and a few others would hold meetings in a village in the Point area. There were very few Christians in this area. The meeting was held in a home of a church elder. At first, the church elder was very reluctant to have the meeting in his home, but finally agreed to it. The meeting began, and the church elder and his wife were the first to fall in a trance. Others started weeping. The elder asked a local deacon to pray. The deacon began to pray, "O Lord! You know that we were praying for revival- but not like this!" (17) Then, the deacon stopped , then started again praising the Lord that although what was happening was unusual, the Spirit of the Lord was present.

It was reported on Friday, May 5, 1939 in the Stornoway Gazette that a meeting took place in the Free Church of Carloway, and that, during the service, several of the worshipers fell into a trance. Similar events took place the following night when a number of the Church of Scotland members were present. The Gazette article reported that "the worshipers have to stand round the doors and windows, unable to gain admittance. The service generally begins about

9 p.m. and continues until the small hours of the morning. When the ministers leave, the meeting is continued mainly with the singing of Psalms, and it is stated that it is during this part of the service that worshipers are generally affected physically. The form, which the revival is taking, is causing a considerable amount of apprehension...."

Rev. M.M. Macsween, the Church of Scotland minister of the Parish of Kinloch, Lewis gave a report at a meeting in Edinburgh in 1939. In this report of the revival on the Isle of Lewis, Macsween said, "The revival was initially confined to the Carloway District. However, this year in a small village to the south side of Loch Erisot, Garyvard, unusual scenes were witnessed. A private house, in which a meeting is being held, actually shook from its foundation and many of those there felt an extraordinary power present and very soon a number of them were physically affected, and fell into what might be termed trances' quietly and without disturbance. Some of them, whom he saw in these trances' seem to be transfigured and in a state of enjoyment. A few of them, who were ready enough to narrate their experience, told how they were conscious of unusual calm and peace, and some had visions. Others could give no account and among those he could see some who were quite prepared to admit that they had experienced no spiritual change. As in every movement of this kind, there were those who were merely affected by the power of social sympathy. In this particular village, however, the movement had influenced for good, and now, when the excitement had cooled down, he found that the people who were influenced lived a normal Christian life, and were very much interested in the Church of Christ and all it stood for. This was not true before. He had attended services in the village with as few as six people present and now he could get anything up to one hundred any time he went. (18)

From Garyvard the revival spread to the villages of Lemraway and Orinsay, then to Crossbost and Grimshader. In all of these places men and women were moved by a strange power, engaging in public prayer and exhortation. They had a deep burden for the salvation of others. Then the movement spread to Barvas. The unusual symptoms followed. Great things were happening everywhere. Although there was a hesitancy to accept many of the things that were happening, the evidence of lasting conversions was happening everywhere.

A very unusual thing: The Revival of 1934-39 had its beginning in the Free Church on the Isle of Lewis in the village of Carloway, and spread to other Free Churches on the island. A later revival in 1949-53 under the preaching of Duncan Campbell had its impact on the Church of Scotland on the island, and this later revival was mostly bitterly opposed by the Free Church clergy. Strange indeed!

The revival movement came to the Shader and Barvas area. These two villages are so close together that they are almost one. It was here that the 1949-53 revival broke out, and now in 1939 the Spirit of God is about to move greatly in these two small villages. As far as I can tell from research, the human instruments leading to revival in Shader and Barvas in 1939 were not ministers , but laymen and laywomen. In the next few pages I would like to tell you of one man and two women who lived and prayed in such a way that God was able to come down on these two wonderful little villages.

JOHN SMITH

John Smith was the blacksmith in the village of Shader. In fact, he was called the "Gobha". Gobha is the Gaelic word for "blacksmith." It is pronounced "Go," Anyone who has done any reading concerning the Revival of 1949-53 will recognize the name of John Smith. John Smith was one of the seven men who met for months in a little barn north of the Barvas Church praying for revival. He was present the night Kenneth Macdonald prayed and the fire of God fell in that little barn. It was John Smith who prayed in a little workshop building in the village of Arnol, "God, did you know your honor is at stake? You promised to pour water on him who is thirsty. Well, God, I am thirsty. If you don't do what you promised, how can I ever believe you again. Did you know your honor is at stake?" When John Smith prayed that prayer, the little workshop building began to violently shake. That night great revival came to the village of Arnol.

This same John Smith was instrumental in the revival of 1934-39 coming to Shader and Barvas. John Smith called the first meetings in Shader in 1939. These meetings were to be held in his home, and it was in his home that revival first broke out in that district.

Early in 1939 there was a Communion Service held in Point, Lewis. Two people were converted to Christ coming home on the bus to Shader. The "Gobha", John Smith, sent word to all the houses in the area that he would be holding a meeting in his home. When the meeting started, John Smith became aware of severe opposition from Satan. He said, "It was so awful that I became convinced that I had been mistaken in holding the meetings and I decided to end them. It took four men to hold me down and prevent me doing this. I was saved in time. That night revival broke out." (19)

Physical manifestations were intense and widespread. People were convicted and converted. Glory flowed down. John Smith discovered that God would mightily work one night and that Satan would rise up and try to destroy the work the next night. In the Shader and Barvas area, some of the greatest opposition came from one of the churches in the area.

MARY MACLEAN

Mary Maclean lived in the village of Balintrushal, near Shader and Barvas. Mary was born in 1905, and was an unusual woman of prayer and commitment to the Lord. When the Revival of 1934-39 came to the Shader and Barvas area in 1939, Mary would have been 34 years of age.

In 1988, Hugh Black, a Pentecostal pastor from Greenock, Scotland visited Mary in her home and interviewed her concerning the revival in her area. The day Hugh Black went to see her, he had not called, written or in any way let her know he was coming, but when he arrived, Mary knew of his coming. She had felt a word from God that he was on his way.

Mary Maclean was a member of the Free Church. She was drawn to the things of God from an early age. She loved being around Christian people, and when elders and deacons would gather in her Grandmother's house, Mary would listen closely to their conversation.

Perhaps, we would do well, and just read the words of Mary as she talked to Hugh Black.

"I remember once, when I was very young, bringing tea to the company when one of the elders asked another if he thought Christians would recognize each other in Heaven. I remember, as though it was yesterday, putting down the cups to hear the answer and thinking how wonderful it would be if the Lord's people would know each other. The second elder thought they would if they had been close to each other on earth. I always envied the Lord's people and wanted to be one of them as far

back as I can remember.

I wasn't interested in the concerts and parties, and I didn't know why I remained so uninterested when other young people were so interested. When I left the co*ncert that night, I knew I would never go to a concert again. There was nothing there for me.*

In those days we used to go out with the cattle to the moor and a girl gave me an English New Testament to read as I had time and quietness. She promised to test me in what I read. This may have encouraged me, but I remember wishing all the time that I was a Christian.

One night a Mr. Macmillan, a missionary, came and one of my cousins was converted and she cried and cried her eyes out. Some people seemed to be so upset as the knowledge of the broken law came on them. I used to envy those people: they were so sure of their conversion. But things weren't like that with me. My own conversion was as though a child was awakened out of sleep. I didn't cry. I wasn't getting law and hard things and I wasn't sure of my conversion. I envied these others and wished I had had an experience like them.

I had a cousin in Glasgow who took me one night to the Highlandman's Umbrella(a famous gathering place for Highland People). I said to myself, If I get out of this, I'll never come back again.' I didn't say it to my cousin, who was older than I , but I was determined that if I got back to Professor Muir's house where I was a cook, I would never visit the Highlandman's Umbrella again.

I attended the Partick Highland Free Church in Glasgow. When church came out it was the custom for the young people to meet on the Great Western Road. A friend met me one night at the door of the church after the service and said, We'll go up to the Great Western Road. Everyone goes there after the meeting.' I didn't like to refuse, although at the time I was seeking the Lord and not getting through. When I got to the Great Western Road, I was ashamed of myself, thinking the boys would be thinking that we were after them. Ah, well', I said, If I get home tonight, I'm not coming here again. I will go straight home after church. I will never go to the Great Western Road again.' When I refused to go with the others they would say, Och, you're converted, you're converted.' I would say, No, I am not converted.' Then why won't you go?' There's nothing there for me. I don't see what interests you there. It has no interest for me, so I won't go.'

It is a wonder I was not burned alive in those days. I would go to bed and , not wanting to have to get up later and put out the gas, I would take a candle and put it on the pillow as I read my Bible and sought God in prayer. One night I fell asleep and when I awoke there was nothing left of the candle but a very small stump. I never did that again.

I had a half-day each week and I wanted to spend this with Christians, but didn't know where to go, and was afraid that if I did find such company I would spoil things for them. Since I was not through to God, I was afraid that I would prevent them getting through too.

One day, as I read my Bible at the part where Christ asks, Are ye come out, as against a robber, with swords and staves to seize me?' , I felt I was like the chief of sinners crucifying Christ. It was five years before I confessed the Lord, going forward to the table for Communion.

The Rev. Peter Chisholm was my minister in Partick Highland Free Church, and he was my favorite preacher. He came down very hard on all forms of sin and I appreciated this. He stirred me and I wanted to be stirred. At last the day came when I got through fully with the Lord. I was on my knees washing the floor when God spoke to me from Ephesians 2:13-14: But now in Christ Jesus ye that once were far off are made night in the blood of Christ, for he is our peace, who made both one, and broke down the middle wall of partition.' I got through on that verse, but then Satan came and said, Nobody ever got through on her knees washing a floor.' That's how I was tempted, it was as if Satan had a grip on my clothes all the time; he said, You're not going to get away.'

Now I had a friend from Lochs, and she came out with me to the Saturday Communion service. She said, Mary, we're going to the session tonight to go forward for Christ.' I said, Jessie Maggie, don't depend on me. The Lord alone knows what I will do tonight. But don't go by me. If you are ready to go into the session, go in, but don't depend on me. Go on your own.

It was Mr. Chisholm who started the service that night, which was unusual since it was his own Communion and normally it was a visiting minister who took the service. I said in my heart, Thank the Lord that it's you that's going to be preaching tonight, and you'll search me thoroughly; you won't leave anything untouched.' So that was that. And as he was going on with the service, at one time I would think, I will go forward....I think I'm getting through all right' and then a wave of doubt would come. In any case, when the service was finished, he said, as everyone says at the end, And those now that want to come forward to the table, the session is open for the last time. And you who are here tonight before me saying that you don't belong to Christ, wherever you put your handwriting, don't say, No', when Christ says, Yes.' And when he said this, he struck his hand on the pulpit. I went past him. I got it there, and I got to a stage when I was no longer worried about what Mr. Chisholm might question me on. I was past thinking of him. I was going forward for Christ that night. It was not the minister now, but Christ. When I went out, there was no sign of my girl-friend, Jessie Maggie. An elder came forward to take me into the session. And all the minister asked was, what had made me come in tonight? And I said I wanted to go as far for Christ as I could. And he didn't ask anything else. He gave me a token and he prayed. You'll now go straight on,' he said. But after I left church, Satan came, Chisholm knew that you had nothing to answer tonight, that's why he didn't put the questions, the deep questions you were thinking he was going to ask. He knew that you had nothing. And the token he gave you tonight, he'll be in the door waiting for you to take it away tomorrow.' I said to Satan, Oh well, God knows I am not worthy of going for Communion. That's all right! That's all right.'

It was on the night after this that I got wonderful light. I had to be in that night, and when I went to sleep, I saw Christ with His hands raised, saying, Father, that which thou has given me, I will that, where I am, they also may be with me.' It was His voice that awoke me, and oh, it was so loud. And when I looked, He was gone. And I didn't know the bedroom; I didn't know where I was. I could only hear singing of birds, and I wasn't hearing trams or cars or anything like that; I didn't know the bedroom at all. And I thought I was going to die; I thought I was going to Heaven.

This was the beginning of vision for me. When I got up, I was still thinking the Lord was going to take me away. And a Christian girl from Ness, from the Church of Scotland, was next door to me. And as soon as I got the dishes washed in the morning, I went round to see her. And she asked me, Oh, Mary, why have you come so early as this?' I said, Oh, Christine, I'm going to die.' She replied, Everyone's going to die. What's wrong, Mary?' I told her of the vision I'd seen of Christ and of the words He spoke to me and the peace I was feeling, and that I was sure I was going to die. She said, You, my dear, go home and do all you have to do. You have to go through a lot before you get away from this world. Go now and do everything you have to do in the house.' And so I did. And the peace was wonderful. It was as if I was walking on air for two years. It was a wonderful time. Jessie Maggie, the girl I told to go forward for Communion if she was ready for it and not go by what I did, waited for another two years. No one went forward that time but myself. This happened when I was twenty-three years old, sixty years ago. I had the presence of the Lord all the time, the power of the Spirit all the time."

This episode from the life of Mary Maclean in Glasgow happened in 1928. She returned to the Isle of Lewis, married, and on March 10, 1939, Mary had a baby daughter. At the birth, she felt herself strongly surrounded by the presence of God. Two nights after the baby was born, her first vision came. Mary told Hugh Black of her vision:

"There came a rushing wind. I was away. I don't know how long I was away, but the graves opened, the graves opened, and I thought it was the last day, Judgment Day. I don't know how long I was away, but when I came back I said, O Lord, if it's Judgment Day, everyone here is unconverted.' And the power came for praying for all those unconverted persons all over the world. The whole world came upon me. And I was shaking, and I prayed that I would go away again. I was just waiting like that. And there came the rushing wind again. I was away. It was the sea that came in front of me then. And I went down to the bottom of the sea. And the ships were lying there, and the bodies of men were lying there. Oh, what a place! I don't know how long I was away, but when I came back I was

shaking, and Baby was beside me. When the war broke out in August, that was when I got a revelation about the place of seeing when I was down at the bottom of the sea and saw the bodies there. I thought, Well, this is the war now that I have seen, the ships down there in pieces, and the bodies.' I was afraid that I would go away again, and wondered what I would see next, what would be revealed to me? But I didn't go away then and decided not to tell anyone of anything I had seen. They would think that the Lord was going to take me away, and they would be so upset.

Now the Communions were coming about the 15th of March, and Baby was born on the 10th. I would preach to the unconverted that a revival was on its way. I told them to be out day and night at the meetings at Communion time and not to miss anything, that a great revival was coming. And, oh, they were thinking something was wrong with me. They didn't know what was coming upon me. Oh, be out, be out morning and night,' I said. Pressure was coming upon me, and prayer was coming. I thought the Lord was going to take me home, and I wasn't worried for the family. I knew the Lord would get someone to look after the family. I was all prepared to be taken away. Oh, the presence of the Lord was so strong. I thought no one could stay in this cold world without the presence of the Lord. And there was a girl who lived near me, and she used to help me with the baby. I used to say, Oh, Hetty, be out morning and evening. Revival's going to come.' And after the Communion, she came and said, I was out every morning and night, and no revival came.' I said, The revival is coming. You keep out. The revival is coming.' Anyway, the Communions in Point came about the end of March. And I was waiting for the revival, when the power would come."

Mary's vision was correct. War was coming, and many of

the young men and women of Lewis would go off to World War II, never to return home again. Her vision of the coming revival was also correct. In fact, it was not far off.

"Two people were converted in the bus coming over from Point to Barvas at the end of the Communions. The Gobha (the Shader blacksmith, John Smith) was there. And when the Gobha got home he sent two wee girls to every house that evening, saying that he was going to hold a meeting, and that he was inviting everyone. My husband wasn't converted at the time. And he was planting potatoes, when he saw the two girls at the door and came up and asked who they were. The Gobha has sent two girls inviting everyone to a meeting in his house tonight.' I said. Oh, yes, but it's not the likes of me the Gobha is inviting, but Christians.' No,' I said, and the pressure came on me, You have to go. You have to go to the meeting.' And when he saw the pressure coming on me, he was afraid and he said, All right, I'll go.' And he went to the meeting that night.

What now about the meeting?' I said, when he came home. One thing about the meeting is that I am thankful you were not out in the meeting." Why?' I said. I know you would have been one of the chief among them. Some were standing singing, some were falling down on the floor, and some others were preaching away, preaching away: and you would have been among them. And I'm thankful you could not go out, that you are not able to be out, with the baby.'

I said, Well, never you mind. All you have to do is close your eyes and leave everything you hear and see and just pray to God, O Lord, open my eyes and gain my heart for yourself.' And ignore everything you hear and see. Don't be offended with anything you see, but pray away for your soul.

He said, "Oh, well, I am thankful you are not among them, and I'm not going tomorrow night.' Yes, you have to go.

You have to go now.' He said, All right. I'll go all right.' He went out that night.

What about the meeting?' I asked, when he came home. When the power came on me in the house here, I was forced to go on my knees. The power of prayer came on me for the meeting, and for the coming of revival to open the hearts of the unconverted. The burden wasn't just for one or two, but for the whole world. My husband said, Oh, they were worse tonight than they were last night. Only I'm thankful that the baby's here to keep you in the house.' That was his story each night, thankful that the baby's here and that you'll not be able to be there.

And the third night, I didn't ask him to go. He went without me asking. When he came home, I didn't venture to ask what was going on. I knew something was happening. I felt it. And when he took the Book, to say prayers, the tears were running down from his eyes, and I never asked about the meeting. I saw that he had been converted.

Another woman in the community, Barbara Macdonald, had been having visions. She too would go away under the power of God. Barbara came to visit Mary:

"But when they heard that I too was under the power, Barbara was allowed in. The power was great. The revival had come.

But Satan came too. Satan had his own power among the people. Oh, yes. When I would send anyone for the young people to come in, I used to preach to them, and when my younger brother came in among the others, he would say, Mary, we don't know who to believe.' The young people were going to the meetings, to Barbara's meeting and to the Gobha's. Some were saying it was the devil's work, and some were saying it was the Lord's. Wasn't it remarkable that some members were saying it was Satan's work? And the poor unconverted souls were standing between the two groups: between Satan and the Lord's work. And that was so hard. And the pressure for prayer for the Church of God came upon us now so heavily; the pressure for the people who were saying it was the devil's work. And there were ministers too against the revival. The minister in our church was against it, but not in the neighboring Church of Scotland. Oh, the battle I have gone through with that minister and the elders. I'll never forget it. But I was standing in the power of the Lord. And I wasn't afraid; I was telling everything that the Lord was doing. And there I was, I had to stay in. But when Baby grew well on in months, I used to go to the Church of Scotland meetings here. War came and my husband went away, and I was here with the family. I wasn't able to go out much, but when I got a chance I would go to the Church of Scotland.

I had then started going into visions again. Some of them were long visions and I needed my mother's help to look after the baby. It wouldn't have been possible for me to attend to her myself, for the length and depth of the visions. The longest vision I've been in was one in which I went cold, as cold as if I were dead. And, oh, the vision I saw there, a vision of Heaven and of hell. And hell, there was a plunging into hell as if sheep were plunging over a precipice, and I was hearing the gnashing of teeth and the crying. I saw the flames going through the people, the flames were not burning up and down the way, but going through them across the way. And I thought, with the furnace that was coming out of hell, that there wasn't a hair on my head that wasn't singed with the furnace.

But, then, a vision of Heaven, and Christ. I couldn't take my eyes off Him. I couldn't blink. And the vision of Heaven was so wonderful. And the brightest day here is like darkness compared with the light that's there in Heaven.

And I was away so far, my sister told my mother, Mary has passed away, and you must believe that Mary won't come back now. She's gone cold, and I have taken out clothes to put on her now, and white sheets that'll go over her in the bed, until the coffin comes.' My sister was so upset. I was just cold, as cold as a dead body. I don't remember now how long my mother said I was away, but a crowd was in the house, thinking that I had passed away and that the wake was going to be on. And there was one in Lower Shader, a very dear soul that was under the power like myself. She was my cousin. And her brother, an elder in the Free Church, was in. And he went home and told her, Annie, you won't see Mary now again. Mary has passed away.' No, I don't believe Mary has passed away. I have often seen Mary going away like this.' Oh, but not like this, Mum. She's stone cold; every bit of her is stone cold, and there's no pulse that we can find.'

Anyway, after that, I don't know how long, but I was a good while away, I felt streams going through my body, through my arms, and through every bit of me, like thin streams warming me up. And when I got a bit warmed up, I said to my sister, Oh, Annie, will you bring me a hot water bottle?' And Annie said that was the most wonderful thing she ever heard. I couldn't move at this stage. I couldn't move my arms or my legs. But bit by bit I was warming up. My right arm warmed first. And when I got as far as putting my arm to my brow, it was like putting a hand on a dead body. My head was still cold. But everything else was warm. And I came back to life.

My mother asked me when she saw I was fully back, Oh, Mary, did you see anything about our own house?' Well, I didn't see anything, but I know this, that you're going to be left alone.'

The war hadn't broken out then. Later my three brothers were taken to the war, and we were left alone then. I have seen that you are going to be alone in the house.' And she couldn't understand how that would happen. Where were the boys going, the three of them? But they were taken to the war in August. And I was with my mother all the time. And it was when the war broke out that I realized that what I had seen in vision down at the bottom of the sea, with the ships and the bodies all about, was connected with the war.

Just before war broke out I was finally able to come home with the children; my husband and my three brothers were taken away to the war. One night I was on my knees praying for my brothers and for everyone in the world. I saw the ship the youngest one was in; it was a trawler. It was in half, it was split in half, and I saw him in the water. With what I saw I got up from my knees and started thinking, Och, it must have been that I was praying for him and was afraid that this would happen.' And I started walking the floor. Oh, what was this? Anyway, word that he was missing came, and I told people that this happened two weeks ago, the night was clear in my memory. The postman left letters here for me to break it to my father and mother. He was missing. But then word came that he wasn't found among the survivors. And I told them, Well, this happened two weeks ago.' They said, How do you know that?' I've seen it. I've seen it with my eyes. I know this.'

Next, my other brother died on board his ship, with, I think, a gastrated stomach. There was a month between them, that was all. And he was buried at sea. Seemingly he had been converted. He had talked to a man from Carloway who was with him on the boat, a Christian. He had said, When we get home after the war, you'll go down to our house, so that it will be easier for me to go out to the weekly meetings with you.'

Soon after that, an urge came on me to go back to my own church, at a Communion time. And I said, O Lord, I can't go there. How can I go there? I have not been going to that church, and how can I venture out at the Communions.' But the pressure of the Lord came, and I had to go. But I wouldn't do this without going first to the elders and saying that I was forced to take Communion.

They said, Oh, well, you'll have to come in before th elders and before the minister.'

Oh, what a position! But mind you, I wasn't afraid. I was going to tell them the truth, and the power that was coming upon me. I wasn't afraid about whether they would turn me back without getting to the Communion table; that wasn't going to worry me. But Christ couldn't say that I didn't go as far as I could. The responsibility would be on them. The minister asked me why I was going out to the Church of Scotland, and wouldn't come to my own church.

Because you wouldn't allow us in there; you wouldn't allow any who were under the power of the Spirit to come in. And I didn't want to spoil anything, or to upset anyone; so I was keeping away from you.'

And do you promise to come if you get to the table?'

Well, I'll promise, if the Lord gives me the strength to come to the church, I'll come. But if not, I can't come.' I also said to the elders, None of you, none of the elders, came to see us during the meetings. And the ministers didn't come to see us during the meetings, during the time when we were under the power of the Spirit. None of you were coming to see us.'

The elders said, Oh, you are right, Mrs. Maclean, none of us went to see you. Well, you'll go forward the same as you ever did.'

And so I did go to the table. But the power came after that, and I couldn't venture out to this church. And at every opportunity I had to go, I went back to the Church of Scotland. And mine you, what a battle; you can understand what I was going through. But the power was so strong from the Lord, and the presence of the Lord was so wonderful, and I was saying, Oh, well, as long as I am under this pressure, the Lord will give me all the words I need. I don't need to worry.' I stayed in at the next Communion. And do you know, I was so much under the power that the Communion bread and wine were brought to me here.

At the next Communion, the Lord's presence and power came strongly and I had to go again. I wasn't afraid, and I was prepared to speak openly to the elders in front of the minister. And the minister asked, Why didn't you come to the church after you had Communion?'

Because when the power came upon me I was going out of the body and I didn't want to upset any of you. When the power of the Spirit came on me, I was going off, and it was there I was seeing the visions.' They made no comment on this. Then said, Oh, well, you can come any time you feel the Lord is leading you to come to the table.' That was my experience with them."

Those of you who have read these words may have some difficulty with them. The experience of Mary Maclean may sound so strange to your ears that you will have trouble accepting them. I realize that the life of a lady like Mary Maclean is so vastly different from our experience with the Lord. With a few on the Isle of Lewis, there seemed to be a very thin veil between them and Heaven. They lived on a different plane, in another atmosphere. They lived and communed with God.

The people of Shader and Barvas were sharply divided during the revival of 1934-39. There were those who were greatly affected by it, and there were others who bitterly opposed the revival. It is interesting that the greatest attack against the revival came from Mary's own church, the Free Church.

During the 1949-53 revival that came to the Isle of Lewis, a young man was converted to Christ on his way to play the bagpipes at a dance. His name was William Smith. He never got to the dance, but went to the church meeting in Barvas, and testified of his conversion to Christ. You might find it interesting that William Smith's wife was Mary Maclean's oldest daughter. (18)

The preacher in the 1949-53 revival on Lewis was the Scottish Highlander preacher, Duncan Campbell. During that great revival, Duncan Campbell was preaching in a house one night. He was finding it very difficult, if not impossible to preach. Campbell stopped, sat down and called on a man named Coinneach Beag to pray. Coinneach stood and began to pray. He prayed for about one-half hour, then he stopped speaking to God, and said, "Will you excuse me for one moment, Lord, while I speak to the devil?" When Duncan Campbell heard this, he opened his eyes and looked at Coinneach. Coinneach had both of his fists raised as a fighting man. Coinneach continued praying, "Devil, on the authority of the shed blood of Jesus Christ, I order you out of this meeting." Suddenly, the power of God fell in the house. Duncan Campbell said the next time he saw Coinneach, he was stretched out on a bench fast asleep. The meeting was still going on, but Coinneach's work was finished and he was sleeping the sleep of the just. Coinneach Beag was the brother of Mary Maclean.(21)

BARBARA MACDONALD

North of the Barvas Church, at the south end of the village of Shader, sits the house of Barbara Macdonald. When I was on the Isle of Lewis in 2001, I sat in a car beside the road for quite some time, looking at the home of Barbara Macdonald, I would then look across the road at the home of John Smith, the Gobha.

Barbara Macdonald was bedridden, and in almost constant pain. During the Revival of 1934-39, Barbara was a holy warrior of prayer.

A man named Colin who lived in the town was an alcoholic. One day he was sitting in a drinking house in Stornoway. He picked up his glass to take a drink, when suddenly Barbara Macdonald stood before him in spirit. Terribly afraid, he put down the glass and started home. When he came down the road and passed Barbara's house, she stepped out in front of him, and he fell to his knees on the road, giving his life to Christ.

While I was sitting in the car beside the road , looking at Barbara Macdonald's home, Donald John Smith, a retired shop-keeper from Shader, was sitting in the car with me. Donald John was converted to Christ during the 1949-53 Revival on the Isle of Lewis. He told me that one night they were in a prayer meeting in the home of Barbara Macdonald. It was late at night, dark as pitch outside, when, suddenly, all around Barbara's house the Shekinah Glory of God shone down, and it became as bright as noonday.

When revival came to Shader and Barvas in 1939, Barbara was unable to attend church because of her health. She spoke of that revival, "Ah, it was a wonderful time, for some people, but for us it was also a terrible time. We were not in the meetings, you know, where the people were being blessed. We were called by God to the place of prayer and we would be in another room when the meetings were going on and the power would come and we would be filled with power and the burden of prayer would grow and grow. It was like childbirth. The pangs would come and the pain would come and then there was a sense of delivery and joy as a soul was born into the kingdom, as was happening in the other room. And then the wind would come again and the pangs and the pain and the delivery. Again and again it would come. It was very wonderful, but it was very costly." (20)

I doubt there are very few, today, who have much acquaintance with this type of intercessory prayer. Lives are so busy today that we have little time to spend with the Lord in deep, agonizing prayer. Church meetings are filled with singing, preaching, announcements, but not much prayer. I, many times, think that great spiritual awakening will never come to our nation until we learn, once again, the secret of being in the closet with God in prayer.

When World War II started, the Revival of 1934-39 on the Isle of Lewis came to a close. Some believe it ceased because so many of the young people of Lewis went to the war. Others believe there was simply a pause in the revival until the close of the war, when revival once again broke out in 1949 in the village of Barvas, and once again began to spread across the island.

It is interesting to note different customs in churches of different cultures. One of the most interesting customs in the churches on the Isle of Lewis is what the churches consider to be the main identifying mark of conversion. At least, it sounds strange to those of us in America.

Across the years, almost all of the people on Lewis would be found in church on Sunday. It was the thing to do. The churches had members and adherents. The adherents were those who attended church, but had never been converted and become members of the church. Most churches had more adherents than members. Across the generations, it became the accepted fact that the demarcation line between those who had been converted, and those who had not, was the weekly prayer meeting. While most went to church on Sunday, only those who had been converted would dare go out to Thursday night prayer meeting. If a person went to prayer meeting, the community would look upon that person as one who had been converted to Christ.

I find it interesting to look at different cultures, different nations and see that which people consider the identifying mark of a Christian.

In 1993 I was on a flight from Oklahoma City to Atlanta, Georgia. I sat down in my assigned seat, and saw that I was seated next to a black man. As we began talking, I was pleasantly surprised to learn he was a black Baptist Pastor from Africa. We talked all the way to Atlanta, Georgia. What an absolutely thrilling conversation! He told me of his conversion, his call to preach, and about the church he served as Pastor. Then, he told me about his childhood. His father was the witch doctor for his tribe. Through the years, he would talk to his father about Jesus Christ, and the father's need of salvation. His words fell on deaf ears. Then, the father fell gravely ill, was dying, and on his deathbed, the father accepted Jesus Christ has his Savior and Lord. The African Pastor said to me, "Do you know how I know that my father was saved? When he prayed to receive Jesus Christ, he began to weep." Then, the Pastor said, "In our culture, when a person weeps, it means that person has committed his life, body and soul, to Jesus Christ. I know my father is in heaven."

In this chapter you have just read, go back again and read the testimony of Murdo Macaulay and Roddy Mackay as they talk about "going out to the prayer meeting." To the person of Lewis, going to prayer meeting meant that your life was to never again be your own, but your life belonged forever to Jesus Christ.

When World War II began, the sun set on the revival of 1934-39 on the Isle of Lewis. It would be a few years before God began to stir the hearts of people again. We would do well to remember that many have said that this revival of 1934-39 was the greatest movement of God that has ever come to the Isle of Lewis.

Rev. John Maciver

Rev. Murdo Macaulay

The Carloway Church

Duncan Macphail

Murdo Macleod
"Murdigan"

John Macleod
"An Cor"

Chapter eight

“THE REVIVAL OF 1949-1953”
(‘DUSGADH 1949-1953)

The spiritual awakening of 1949-53 that came to the Isle of Lewis has come down through church history to be known as the Lewis Revival. That term is true, however, there have been other Lewis Revivals, great revivals in which God has come to make Himself known.

It has been my privilege to research the revival of 1949-53 and to write a book concerning it. This book, *Catch the Wind*, was released in 2002. One of the great spiritual blessings of my life has been the writing of this book; the study, the searching, then in October, 2001 I made a trip to the Isle of Lewis to interview elderly people who were converted to Christ during this great revival. What a blessing!

It seems in every great revival movement throughout church history, a Scripture would rise to the surface, and become almost the motto of that revival movement. It was as if there was a certain truth God wanted to emphasize at a certain time and a certain place. For instance, in the Reformation in Europe in the 1500's, the Scripture that rose to the surface was the one that says, "The just shall live by faith." (See Habakkuk 2:4, Romans 1:17, Hebrews 10:38)

In the great spiritual movement in England under the preaching of John Wesley and George Whitfield, the Scripture that rose to the surface was the one that says, "Ye must be born again" (John 3:7). In fact, history tells us that George Whitfield preached on this text over 500 times. A friend once asked Whitfield, "Why do you preach on that text so much?" Whitfield replied, "Because, ye must be born again."

In the Lewis Revival of 1949-53, two Scriptures rose to the surface, and became the motto of that great revival. The first, "Who shall ascend to the hill of the Lord? Who shall stand in His holy place? He who has clean hands and a pure heart, who has not lifted up his soul to vanity, nor sworn deceitfully, he shall receive the blessing from the Lord" (Psalms 24:3-5). The other Scripture, "I will pour water upon him who is thirsty, and floods upon the dry ground" (Isaiah 44:3).

The Revival of 1949-53 came directly from God, but, on this earth, there were two principals who were busily at work, bringing the heart of God to the Isle of Lewis. The preacher during this revival was the Scottish Highlander, Duncan Campbell. He was a work in progress for God to use in a mighty, unusual way. The other principal in the revival was a group of seven men, and two elderly women on the Isle of Lewis that God was to fill and use in a wonderful, gracious way.

Duncan Campbell was born in 1898 six miles north of Oban, Scotland, the son of Hugh and Jane Campbell. He was converted to Christ at the age of 15, falling under conviction one night while playing the bagpipes during a Scottish dance. Duncan went home that night, made his way to the barn, and prayed, "O God, I know not how to come. I know not what to do, but, my God, I'm coming now. Have mercy on me." (1)

Perhaps the most defining moment in the life of Duncan Campbell was on the battlefield in France during World War I. Campbell was nineteen years of age when he was badly wounded in a Calvary charge. He was picked up off the battlefield by a Canadian cavalrymen, who threw him behind his saddle. On that horse's back, Campbell prayed a prayer he had heard his father pray, "Oh God, make me as holy as a saved sinner can be!" (2)

Throughout the rest of his life, Duncan Campbell called this experience on the horse's back by different names. Sometimes he referred to it as, "full salvation." Other times he would call it, "being filled with the Holy Spirit." Most of the time he would say he was, "baptized with the Holy Ghost." Whatever name that was applied to this experience, Duncan Campbell learned the secret of the Spirit-filled life. He spent five years as a pilgrim with the Faith Mission organization, working in the Argyll area of Scotland where he grew up. He would walk around the country-side talking about Jesus Christ.

In 1923, at the age of 25, Duncan Campbell became a church Minister. He served as a Minister for 24 years in three different churches. He first served in the village of Ardvasar on the Isle of Skye, then in the town of Balintore on the Northeast coast of the mainland of Scotland, then he went to Falkirk, a city in the center of the nation of Scotland.

For twenty-four years, Duncan Campbell served as a church Minister, but in his own words, "I came under the influence of professors that did not believe in the authority nor the inspiration of the Word of God. I found myself doubting the first three chapters of Genesis. Now, it's true that I was evangelical in my preaching. I was called on to preach in special missions. I was a popular Keswick Convention speaker, because I was Campbell of the Argyll Revival, but I was moving in a barren wilderness." (3)

The pivotal point in Duncan Campbell's life came on November 15, 1947. Campbell is now forty-nine years of age. Early one morning he is in his upstairs study in the manse in Falkirk when he hears singing coming from the parlor downstairs. He immediately recognizes the voice of his sixteen-year-old daughter, Sheena. Campbell walked downstairs, entered the parlor, sat down and listened while Sheena finished singing. Something stirred in Campbell's heart as he listened to his little daughter sing. She sat down on Campbell's lap and said, "Daddy, for several days I have been battling against asking you a question, but I must do it. Daddy, when you were a young Pilgrim with the Faith Mission, you saw revival. Daddy, why is it not with you now, as it once was? Daddy, how is it that you are not seeing revival now?" Then Sheena hit her father with a crushing question, "Daddy, you have a large congregation and many are joining the church, but, when did you last kneel beside a poor sinner and lead him to Jesus?" (4)

That question shook Duncan Campbell to the depths of his soul. When he returned from preaching at a Keswick Convention, he announced to his wife, Shona, and his daughter, Sheena, "I am going to my study. I will not be out to eat or to drink until I am right with God." (5)

That night in his study, Duncan Campbell, almost fifty years of age, came back to the fullness of the Holy Spirit. He said his experience in his study was just like the experience he had had on horse's back in France during World War I. God came into his life in all of His fullness. Campbell resigned his church, and, once again, became a Pilgrim with the Faith Mission, preaching on the Isle of Skye.

There are about 500 islands in the group known as the Hebrides Islands. Lewis is the largest of the islands. Lewis is also the most northern of all the islands.

In 1949, the Church Presbytery met in the village of Ness, on the north end of the island. The Presbytery drafted a declaration deploring the low state of religion on the island. The declaration went on to name the concern of the low state of religion among the young people of the island. The Presbytery voted that this declaration was to be read from the pulpit of the churches on the Isle of Lewis the next Sunday morning.

At this time, the minister of the church in the village of

Barvas was the Rev. James Murray Mackay. James Murray Mackay had been church minister on the mainland of Scotland. Because of the lack of Gaelic-speaking preachers, an appeal was made early in 1949 for any Gaelic-speaking preachers to give some time to the churches on the Isle of Lewis. Mackay went to the church in Barvas for one month. When he returned home, he could not get the Barvas church out of his mind. He felt in his own heart that the Barvas Church was very close to revival. He longed to be a part of it. In April, 1949, James Murray Mackay was installed as Minister of the Barvas Church, eight months before God came down in all of His glory on that church. (Would you permit me to pause in my writing here, and relate a wonderful blessing? I am writing these words on April 12, 2004. Two weeks ago I received a wonderful, surprising letter in the mail. I received a letter from Mrs. Elizabeth Mackay, the widow of James Murray Mackay. I had no idea she was still living. It was a sweet gracious letter. Mrs. Mackay wrote of the great blessing of the revival. She said it was a time when God was walking through the land in a marvelous way.)

On the following Sunday morning, Mr. Mackay read the declaration from the pulpit of the Barvas Church. The next day, Monday, he went to the home of two elderly sisters who were unable to attend church because of their health. Mackay went to their home to read the declaration to them. The two sisters were, Peggy Smith, 84, who was almost totally blind; and her sister, Christine Smith, 82, who was almost bent double with arthritis.

After hearing the declaration read by their minister, the two sisters committed themselves to God in prayer. They lifted up their voices to the Lord in their native Gaelic. A few days later, the sisters called for Mr. Mackay to return to their home.

Peggy told him of a vision that the Lord had given to her. She saw the church of her fathers (the Barvas Church) filled with people, especially young people. There came to the two sisters the promise of God, "I will pour water upon him that is thirsty, and floods upon the dry ground." (Isaiah 44:3)

When the sisters relayed this vision to Mr. Mackay, he asked, "What do you think we should do?"

Peggy Smith replied, "What? Give yourselves to prayer! Give yourselves to waiting on God! Get the elders together, your deacons together, and spend at least two nights a week waiting on God in prayer. If you will do that at the other end of the parish, my sister and I will get down on our knees here in our home from 10:00 at night until 2:00 or 3:00 in the morning." (6)

Mr. Mackay got six men of the church. I have searched and searched through the years, and have only been able to identify four of the men; Kenneth Macdonald, Roderick Macleod, John Smith and Donald Morrison. John Smith was the "Gobha", the blacksmith of Shader who was such an important figure in the revival of 1934-39.

The minister, Mr. Mackay, and the six men found a little barn north of the Barvas Church in which they could pray. For months, they prayed in that little barn, and Peggy and Christine Smith prayed in their humble little cottage. They would pray Tuesday and Friday night, from 10:00 at night until 2:00 or 3:00 in the morning. They prayed for over three months, waiting on God.

THEN, one night, in that little barn, Kenneth Macdonald, who was a deacon in the Barvas Church, rose to his feet in that little barn. He opened his Bible and read a portion of Psalm 24, "Who shall ascend to the hill of the Lord? Who shall stand in His holy place? He that has clean hands and a pure heart, who has not lifted up his soul unto vanity, nor sworn deceitfully, he shall receive the blessing of the Lord." (Psalm 24:3-5)

Kenneth Macdonald then closed his Bible, looked to heaven, and said, "It seems to me just so much humbug to be waiting as we are waiting, and praying as we are praying, if we ourselves are not rightly related to God." Then, he lifted both hands toward heaven, and cried out, "O God, are my hands clean, is my heart pure?" Then Deacon Macdonald fell on his knees in the straw, and in a moment he fell into a trance, unconscious. (7)

That night, revival came to the Isle of Lewis. Following events are difficult to place on paper, for they are wonderful, inspiring, and beyond mere words to describe.

Before I come to the invitation of Duncan Campbell to come to the Isle of Lewis and preach, I think it would be right and proper to address a deep concern of Campbell's. On one occasion, years after the Lewis Revival of 1949-53, Duncan Campbell arrived at the place where he was to preach, and found himself advertised as "The Man Who Brought Revival to the Hebrides." He was extremely upset. He said that revival was a sovereign act of God, and that revival had come to the Isle of Lewis before he ever arrived. Campbell said, "I did not bring revival to Lewis. It grieves me to read or hear people talk about the man who brought revival to Lewis. I thank God for the privilege of being there, and, in some small measure leading the movement for about three years, but God moved in the parish of Barvas before I ever set foot on the island." (8) In fact, the letter I received from Mrs. Elizabeth Mackay, the widow of the Barvas minister, James Murray Mackay, mentions that revival had come to the lives of several people before Duncan Campbell arrived.

The fire of God had fallen in a prayer meeting in a little barn, north of the Barvas Church. Mr. Mackay told Peggy and Christine Smith of this experience. About three days later, Peggy Smith called for her minister to come to their home again. She told him that they had been in prayer. God had given her a vision. God had told her that revival was coming, and He had told her the name of the human instrument that He would use. Peggy said to Mr. Mackay, "God has given me a vision. He gave me a message to give to you. God told me to tell you to invite a preacher named Duncan Campbell to come to Barvas and preach a mission (meeting). I don't know who Duncan Campbell is. I had never heard his name until God told me. God said Duncan Campbell would be here within a fortnight (two weeks)." (9)

Rev. Mackay got in touch with Duncan Campbell who was preaching on the Isle of Skye. He invited him to come to Barvas, but Campbell said it was impossible for him to come. He was planning a convention on Skye, but he would try to come to Barvas the next year.

Mackay returned to Peggy and Christine Smith's home to tell them the bad news. Duncan Campbell could not come. Peggy Smith replied, "That's what man says. God has said otherwise! God told me he would be here in a fortnight." (10)

The convention Duncan Campbell was planning was cancelled because of a series of circumstances. He got in touch with Rev. Mackay, and said he could come to Barvas. He rode the ferry from the Isle of Skye to the Isle of Lewis. He was met at the dock by Rev. Mackay and a church elder.

It is good to remember, at this point, that Duncan Campbell had been invited to come to preach a ten-day meeting at the Barvas Church. There was no newspaper advertising, no handbills printed, no publicity of any kind.

The only thing that had been done; an announcement had been made from the pulpit that a preacher named Duncan Campbell would be coming to Barvas to preach a ten-day meeting. Duncan Campbell came to Barvas for ten days, he didn't go home for almost three years. Why? Because God came down in all of His Glory!

Because of what happened that night at the church, it is good to know something of the worship style of the churches of Lewis. The music is vastly different than our music in American churches. Even to this day, there are no musical instruments in the churches. There are no hymns sung, no gospel songs. The only songs sung in the churches on the Isle of Lewis are the Psalms, sung from the Scottish Metrical Verse. The elected church leader who is charge of the music is called, the Presentor. He stands, presents (announces the Psalm), begins the singing, then sits down.

That night, about 300 people gathered for the church service. Three hundred is about the capacity for the church building in Barvas. They had prayers, sang psalms, and Duncan Campbell spoke. He said it was a very ordinary service. He pronounced the benediction, the people moved out of the building, and stopped in the front church yard. They did not go home. They were not standing outside visiting. They were standing there in a tense silence. Duncan Campbell left the pulpit, walking up the aisle toward the front door of the church, when Kenneth Macdonald, the deacon who had prayed the prayer in the little barn, came up to him. Macdonald said, "Mr. Campbell, God is hovering over us, and He is going to break through in a mighty move." (11) Kenneth Macdonald fell to his knees in the aisle, and began to pray, then fell into the aisle, and went into another trance. The Session Clerk of the church came in the front door, and said,

"Come to the church door and see what is happening!" Duncan Campbell went to the front porch of the church, and the crowd of 300 that had been in the church service had now swelled to over 600 people. Where had they come from? The Spirit of God had fallen on the homes of the village of Barvas. The people had left their homes and made their way to the front yard of the church. There was a big dance in the community that night. The Holy Spirit had fallen on the dance. They had dismissed, and now, the dancers are standing in front of the church.

A church elder asked Duncan Campbell, "What shall we do?" Campbell suggested they all sing Psalm 126. The crowd began to sing:

When Zion's bondage God turned back,
As men that dreamed were we.
Then filled with laughter was our mouth,
Our tongues with melody:
They mong the heathen said, The Lord
Great things for them hath wrought.
The Lord hath done great things for us,
Whence joy to us is brought.
As streams of water in the south,
Our bondage, Lord, recall,
Who sow in tears, a reaping time
Of joy enjoy they shall.
That man who, bearing precious seed,
In going forth doth mourn,
He doubtless, bringing back his sheaves,
Rejoicing shall return.

When they finished singing the Psalm, the crowd flooded back into the church house. Only about one-half of the crowd could get into the church. Duncan Campbell came back into the church. Every available space was taken. People were sitting in the window sills, lying in the aisle, weeping and crying out to God. When Campbell made his way to the pulpit, there was a young lady, a local school teacher, who was lying on the pulpit steps, weeping and crying out to God, "O God, is there any mercy for a sinner like me?" (12) This young lady had been at the dance, and was now at the church. You might be interested to know that there was mercy for her. She was converted to Christ, and spent the rest of her life as a missionary in Nigeria. (13)

Duncan Campbell attempted to preach, but found it futile. No one could hear him, because of all the weeping and the people crying out to a holy God. He finally stepped aside, and just watched God work in the lives of the people.

At 3:00 in the morning, Campbell decided to go home. He was staying in the home of the minister, Rev. Mackay. Campbell and Rev. Mackay went home. Some have found that very interesting. In America, the preacher is supposed to stay and counsel with each individual, but, in Barvas, the preachers left. Duncan Campbell said, "We just left the church filled with people, crying out to God. We left them for God to deal with. God is the supreme counselor. They might not find God that night, nor the next, nor next week, nor next month, but, if they are seeking God with all their hearts, they will find Him. We gave no invitation. We did not say, Come to Jesus and be happy.' A person under deep conviction of sin is not happy." (14)

On the way to the minister's home, a young man came running up to Duncan Campbell and asked Campbell to go down south of the church to the police station. He said there was a large crowd of people in front of the police station, weeping and crying out to God. Who were these people? These were all the people who were standing in the church yard, who could not get back into the church. Campbell walked to the police station, and found the people standing, kneeling, lying in the roadway in front of the police station.

All the time I was doing research on this great revival, I would come across this time when the people left the church yard and made their way to the police station. It did not make sense to me. I could not understand it. Why would the people leave the church yard, and go to the police station? I did not understand until I went to the village of Barvas. The people were not in front of the police station. Just next door to the police station was the humble, little cottage of Peggy and Christine Smith. The people of Barvas understood where the seat of divine power was. They had come to kneel in front of the home of two elderly sisters who knew God.

After that night at the Barvas Church, a power was let loose on the Isle of Lewis. This power of God spread. The following headline appeared in the island newspaper, "The Spirit of the Lord was resting wonderfully and graciously on the different townships the following morning. You could feel His presence in the homes of the people, on meadows and moorland, and even in walking the public roads. God appears to be everywhere." (15)

The revival continued in the village of Barvas, and then leaped to the village of Ness on the north end of the island. One night, word came to Duncan Campbell that the church in Ness was crowded at 1:00 in the morning. When Campbell arrived at the church, he found it packed with people, others were standing outside. Campbell spoke, then invited any who were interested in being saved to come to a meeting in a home. These home meetings came to be called, "kitchen meetings." That night, the kitchen meeting in Ness dismissed at 3:00 in the morning. Campbell then found a large crowd of 300 people out in a field who had been unable to get into the church. He spoke to them. As he made his way home that night, Campbell saw something that made a deep impression on him. A man was lying on the ground. Three teen-age girls were kneeling beside him. One of the girls said to the man, "The Jesus who saved us last night can save you now." The three girls saw that man saved that night. (16)

Stories of what happened on the Isle of Lewis during this great revival are so numerous that I cannot put them all in this book. I have included many of the stories in my book, *Catch the Wind*, but will only share with you a few of my favorite stories in this book.

THE STORY OF ARNOL

About four miles south of the village of Barvas is the village of Arnol. Revival had not come to this village, probably because a minister in this village was very much opposed to the revival. His opposition had to do with doctrine. It was felt that Duncan Campbell talking about the baptism of the Holy Ghost was not according to the confession of faith of their church. In fact, ministers from all over the island came to Arnol in May, 1950 to hold a position meeting. The people were going to this position meeting, but were not going to Barvas to the revival services.

A small little building was found in Arnol for Duncan Campbell and some of the "Praying Men of Barvas" to go and pray. That night the prayer meeting was very difficult. The prayers were stiff and formal, no fire, no vision.

After midnight, Duncan Campbell asked John Smith to pray. John Smith, the "Gobha", the blacksmith of Shader, must have been a most remarkable man. He was a man who knew God, and who knew how to get in touch with God.

John Smith began to pray. He prayed for about thirty minutes, then stopped. He raised both hands to heaven and prayed, "God, do you know that your honor is at stake? You promised to pour water on those who are thirsty, and floods upon the dry ground. God, I don't know where these other men stand with you. I don't know where Duncan Campbell stands with you, but, if I know my own heart, God, I am thirsty and you promised that you would pour water on the thirsty and floods on the dry ground. O God, if you don't do it, how can I believe you again? O God, on the basis of Christ's atonement, I challenge you to fulfill your covenant engagement and do it now. God, your honor is at stake." (17)

At that moment, that little meeting house began to violently shake. Some of the men thought an earthquake had come, but it reminded Duncan Campbell of Acts 4:31, "And when they had prayed, the place where they were assembled together was shaken; and they were all filled with the Holy Spirit, and they spoke the word of God with boldness."

Duncan Campbell immediately dismissed the prayer meeting, because he knew "that God had taken the field." The men walked out into the night in the village of Arnol. It was 2:00 in the morning. They watched as lights began to come on in the houses of Arnol. Men and women began to walk toward the little meeting house, carrying chairs, stools and torches, asking if there was room for them at the meeting. Revival came to Arnol that night. What a visitation of God it was!

THE STORY OF DONALD MACPHAIL

During the first week of revival in the village of Arnol, a young 15-year-old boy was saved. His name was Donald Macphail. In his own testimony, Donald Macphail said he was converted to Christ in a meeting being conducted in a home at

28 Arnol. When I was in Arnol in October, 2001, I had the privilege of speaking to an elderly gentleman, Donald Macleod. He told me of his conversion to Christ during this great revival in Arnol. The home I was sitting in was 28 Arnol, the very house where Donald Macphail found eternal life in Jesus Christ. Two weeks after he was converted to Christ, he was out among the heather in prayer, and God filled Donald Macphail with the Holy Spirit. Duncan Campbell said of this teen-age boy that he was closer to God than any other person he had ever known.

One day, Duncan Campbell went to the Macphail home. Donald's mother told Campbell that Donald was out in his usual place. He was in the barn, praying. Campbell went out to the barn, cracked the barn door, and saw Donald Macphail on his knees in the corner of the barn. When the barn door opened, Donald Macphail looked up, saw Duncan Campbell, and said, "Mr. Campbell, would you excuse be for a bit? I am having an audience with the King." (18)

On another occasion, Duncan Campbell received a letter from a man on Lewis who was an avowed communist. In the letter, the man was castigating the revival, denying God. Campbell went to the man's home to visit him. The man asked Campbell, "Can you prove to me, logically, that there is a God?" Campbell replied, "No! The God in whom I believe you cannot know by logic. You can only know him by faith." Campbell continued, "If you want to know the God in whom I believe, I challenge you to go to the village of Arnol, and spend a half-a-day."

A few days later, Campbell received a call from the man, who asked him to come back to his home. When Campbell entered, he could see the light of Jesus Christ in the man's eyes. The man told Campbell, "You were wrong! You were wrong! You told me to go and spend a half-day in Arnol. Half an hour was enough! I ran into Donnie Macphail!" (19)

The year was 1951. It was the second year of revival on the Isle of Lewis. Off the southwest coast of the Isle of Lewis is the island of Bernera. Duncan Campbell was invited to come to the island of Bernera to preach Communion Services. When he arrived, he found the preaching very difficult. In fact, he found it almost impossible to preach. The revival had not come to this island.

Campbell called a weaver in Barvas, a man who knew how to pray. Campbell asked the weaver if he would get a group of the praying men of Barvas together and come to the island of Bernera to pray? Campbell then told the weaver, "If you can, bring little Donnie Macphail with you." Donald Macphail was now 16 years of age.

When the men arrived with Donald Macphail, they had a time of devotion. In the Scripture reading, they read from the Book of Revelation where John had a vision of heaven opening up before him, and he saw God sitting on His throne.

That night the service began. Campbell began to preach, but felt bound and fettered. He looked down and saw Donald Macphail sitting on the front row, weeping, the floor in front of him was wet with his tears. Duncan Campbell stopped preaching, and said, "Donald, you are nearer to God than I am. I want you to pray."

Little Donnie Macphail began to pray. He prayed for twenty or thirty minutes, when, all of a sudden, he stopped praying, lifted his hands toward heaven, and said, "God, I seem to be gazing in through an open door. I see the Lamb in the midst of the throne with the keys of death and hell." At this point Donnie Macphail is sobbing his heart out. He lifted his hands back to heaven and said, "My God, I see power there, let it loose!"

He said it a second time, "My God, I see power there, let it loose!"

THEN THE FIRE OF GOD FELL! Duncan Campbell was never able to explain the physical manifestations that then occurred. Campbell only said that what happened next was the only time in all of his life he ever saw it. All of the people on Campbell's right threw their two hands into the air, toward heaven, fell back in their pews, and remained in a rigid state for two hours. All of the people on Campbell's left just slumped into each other on the pews, weeping and crying out to God. They stayed that way for two hours. (20)

God swept in that night. God swept into a small village five miles away, at the same time He swept into the church. That night, there was not a house in this village, five miles away, where someone was not saved while little Donnie Macphail was praying.

When Donald Macphail grew up, he went out and spent his life as a missionary among the Muslims in the nation of Yemen. Today, Donald Macphail is retired and once again living on the Isle of Lewis in the town of Stornoway.

THE STORY OF HECTOR MACKENNON

Duncan Campbell received an invitation to preach at a convention in Bangor, Ireland in 1951.Campbell was sitting on the platform in Ireland, the night before he was to preach the closing sermon. Suddenly, he felt that deep, abiding presence of the Holy Sprit inside. The Spirit of the Lord was telling him to go to Greater Bernera, and to go immediately.

Greater Bernera is an island off the southwest coast of Lewis in the Loch Roag. Greater Bernera had a very small population. Duncan Campbell had never been to this island. He did not know anyone living on this island.

Campbell went to the chairman of the convention and

told him that he had to leave. Campbell told him that he had to go right then. The chairman reminded Campbell that he was to preach the closing message the next night. Campbell simply told the chairman that the Holy Spirit had told him to go, and he must obey.

The next morning, Campbell took a plane to Glasgow, then another plane to Stornoway. He then had someone drive him to the southwest coast of Lewis, where he found a man with a small row boat who took him out to the island of Greater Bernera.

When Duncan Campbell stepped on the dock, a boy of eight or nine years old was standing there. Campbell asked the boy to go to their minister and tell him that Duncan Campbell was there. The boy replied, "We don't have a minister. We have two churches, but neither one has a minister at this time. Elder Hector Mackennon is in charge of the church, and he lives in that house on the hill."

Campbell said to the boy, "You go tell Elder Mackennon that Duncan Campbell is here, and if he asks what Duncan Campbell , tell him the Duncan Campbell of the Lewis Revival." The little boy ran off, and returned in a bit, and said, "Elder Mackennon said to tell you he was expecting you. You are to stay with his brother, and Elder Mackennon has already called a meeting at the church at 9:00 tonight, and you are preaching." (21)

Later that day, Duncan Campbell found out the full story of what had happened from Hector Mackennon's wife. Hector Mackennon was the island postman. The day before, when Duncan Campbell had been on the platform in Bangor, Ireland, Hector Mackennon had spent the day in his barn in prayer. Three times his wife had gone to the barn to check on him. Each time she went, her husband was praying the same prayer, "God, I don't know where he is, but You know. God, send him to us." At 10:00 at night, Hector Mackennon felt a peace come over him, a peace that God had answered his prayer. This was the same time that Duncan Campbell had felt the stirring of the Holy Spirit in his heart, telling him to go to Greater Bernera.

The church on Greater Bernera is located just outside the village, at the top of a little hill. Duncan Campbell made his way to the church that night. They had a very ordinary service; singing of psalms, prayers, and Campbell preached. Nothing unusual occurred.

Campbell pronounced the benediction, and the people started their walk back down the hill toward the village. Duncan Campbell and Hector Mackennon were standing on the front porch of the church. Mackennon suddenly took off his hat, stood at attention, and said, "Mr. Campbell, stand! God has come!"

Campbell and Mackennon watched down the hill as the people began to fall, by the roadside and into the heather, crying out to God for mercy.

When the people were able, they made their way back up the hill, into the church. That service lasted until 5:00 in the morning. Campbell was only able to stay on that small island for five days, but it was five days of wonderful revival. Duncan Campbell said there was not a home on the island where someone was not converted to Christ.

We should well remember Hector Mackennon, the Postman of Greater Bernera. His prayer to God that He send Duncan Campbell to their island was no trivial matter. For a long time it had been Mackennon's habit to go to the seashore, behind a big rock and pray.

FOURTEEN YOUNG MEN WHO NEVER ORDERED THE WHISKEY

Early one morning at 5:00, Duncan Campbell was on his way to visit a young minister in a village where the revival had not yet come. Campbell had known this young minister in college in Edinburgh. On the way to the church on his motor bike, Campbell encountered a young woman of 25 years of age kneeling beside the road. He stopped to help her, but found that she was praying. She and two teen-age girls had been praying for several months for revival to come to their village.

On this night the three young ladies had been meeting in prayer. One of the teen-age girls had received the assurance that God was about to send revival. Campbell and the young lady prayed beside the road for three hours. Campbell went on to the manse to visit the young minister. When he arrived, the young minister came out to meet him, completely astounded. That morning, fourteen young men had met in the road in front of the church, discussing the amount of whiskey to order for a concert and dance to be held in the village on Friday night. As they discussed this, one of the young men said, "Boys, I think we should increase the amount of whiskey, because I have a strange feeling that this is the last time whiskey is going to come to this parish."

Another of the young men said, "Angus, surely you aren't suggesting that revival is coming, that we are going to see what they are seeing on the other side of the island.?"

Angus replied, "I don't know what is happening, but something is happening in my heart right now." Angus fell to his knees and began to cry for mercy from God. Within one hour, all fourteen of the young men had been converted to Christ.

Duncan Campbell stayed in this parish for six weeks. He said it was like being in the midst of glory.

Fourteen years later, Duncan Campbell returned to this church to preach one Sunday. After the service, he was introduced to the eleven elders of the church. Ten of the elders were these young men who had been discussing the order of whiskey when they were suddenly captivated by God.(22)

I came across an interesting story concerning Duncan Campbell in 2003. I was preaching a Spiritual Awakening Conference in eastern Oklahoma. A Pastor in a neighboring church attended the services one evening, and told me the following story. In 1968, this Pastor was a late teen-ager. His father took him to the Milldale Bible Conference in Milldale, Louisiana. Duncan Campbell was one of the preachers. One night this young man and his father were seated right behind Duncan Campbell and another man. The moderator of the meeting that night called on an American evangelist to come to the stage and lead in prayer. This evangelist was quite well known. Shortly after the Bible conference ended, the world of this evangelist came tumbling down. All the truth came out about him embezzling money, and gross unfaithfulness in his marriage. That night at the Bible conference, when the evangelist walked to the pulpit, Duncan Campbell turned to the man seated beside him, and asked, "Who is that?" The man replied, "That is so-and-so, a famous evangelist in America. Why?" Duncan Campbell said, "Because, when he walked up on stage, the Holy Spirit walked off."

What spiritual sensitivity! What discernment Duncan Campbell had! And, it was because he was filled with the Holy Spirit.

The stories of the Lewis Revival of 1949-53 could go on and on and on. God simply came down, in all of His Glory, and gripped an entire island for Himself. The atmosphere glittered with divine life. The people would talk about everything containing the presence of the Living God; the rocks, the heather, the sea, the animals. Everything was crying out that God was present. It is reminiscent of the day when the Pharisees asked Jesus to rebuke his followers for praising Him. Jesus said, "I tell you that, if these should hold their peace, the rocks would immediately cry out" (Luke 19:40).

Every small item became a vehicle for bringing men and women to Jesus Christ. During the Lewis Revival an old, hardened sinner was sitting at a table. He began watching a fly buzzing around a lamp. He watched the fly for some time, muttering under his breath, "If you go any closer, you'll get burned." These thoughts began to flash across his soul. He suddenly thought of the danger his own soul was facing, and he began to seek the Lord. (23)

I find it so difficult to place these words on paper. I sit here thinking of the totally inadequate job I am doing of trying to put the workings of Almighty God on a computer. How does one describe the coming of the Glory of God? How does one put into words the dealings of the Holy Spirit with a man, woman, or young person? How does one convey a deep, eternal meaning in a life that is turned from sin to salvation in Jesus Christ? One doesn't! One just sits and praises a God who will come into a life, and, by grace, change that person into a new creation.

In the Revival of 1934-39, the village of Carloway experienced a great movement of the hand of God. In the Revival of 1949-53, God once again came in great power on the village of Carloway. During this revival, the minister of the church in Carloway was the Rev. Murdo Maclennan. He was a man who had a great heart for revival. The Spirit of God had fallen on the Barvas Church on December 11, 1949. At a business meeting in the Carloway Church on December 25, 1949, there is recorded one of greatest plans for revival I have ever seen in my life. As a Pastor for many years, I have read countless plans for revival, systems and ways to engage the Spirit of God, but when I first read the plan laid out by the Rev. Murdo Maclennan, I thought to myself, "This is it! This is it!"

The Carloway Church met on Sunday, December 25, 1949 for a business meeting. Rev. Maclennan said, "Thank God for the success of the Barvas Campaign. For some years I have been trying to get Rev. Duncan Campbell to assist at our communion, but he was engaged on all occasions and was sorry he could not come. Now that the Lord has opened the door, in a marvelous way, I have secured his services for a special evangelistic campaign in February. Until then there are about six weeks, almost the time that the disciples waited in the upper room, on their return from Olivet, for the promise of the Father. Six weeks of prayer until the day of Pentecost was fully come; then suddenly the Holy Spirit came upon them like a rushing, mighty wind and in cloven tongues of fire.

SO, to your knees, God's people! Remember the stone-breaker by the roadside who said, 'I break them on my knees!' This kind goeth not forth but by prayer and fasting. Therefore you must take this to heart. Before you will receive a full blessing, the following conditions must be met:

1. First and foremost, God's glory from first to last!
2. Confession of, and putting away of all known sin!
3. Full dedication to God of our bodies and spirits so that we may become channels of blessing.
4. Absolute faith and utter dependence on the power of God to raise the dead (spiritually)

5. Prayer and intercession day and night on behalf of: Duncan Campbell, that God would use him in the salvation of precious souls That he will come in the fullness of the blessing of the gospel of Christ That he will be kept in health and strength.

If these conditions are fulfilled, I will guarantee you that God will open the windows of heaven to pour out His blessing, and there shall be no room to contain it. (24)

The Lewis Revival of 1949-53 began to subside in its intensity. Duncan Campbell stayed on Lewis for almost three years. In 1953, the intense glory of the revival began to fade.

I have had countless people ask me, "Why did the revival stop? Why didn't it keep going on and on?"

We should remember that even Pentecost did not keep going on and on. Rev.Allan Ian Macarthur, who was converted to Christ during the Lewis Revival of 1949-53, said this, "Revival doesn't go on forever. History shows us that it comes in phases and then dies out. The Spirit of God may be bruised by man's ideas, wounded by men. On Lewis, people became jealous in particular lives, in a particular church. There were occasions where there were those who were all for what God was doing in the beginning, and they turned completely against it in the end." (25).

In all of the study of the revival of 1949-53, the thing that touched me most was the thin veil between earth and heaven. To some of those wonderful believers on Lewis, it seems as if they could be walking on earth one moment, and be stepping into heaven the next. They moved back and forth, living in the glory of the Living God. To many, it was the mere parting of a curtain, a small step into the things of God. One of the most touching statements I have read was made by Chirsty Maggie Macleod, who was saved during this great revival. At the time of her conversion, she was a young person. She said, "At a point of desperation, something happened that I have never been able to explain. It seemed as if a cool breeze went through the room, and I heard a clear voice say, 'Jesus of Nazareth passeth by.' It was so real that I put out my hand to touch Him and He saved me in that instant. The presence of God in that room was so real. Joy welled up within me, and I knew that I was His." (26)

No one knows the mind and purpose of God. No one understands why the Wind begins to blow, where the Wind comes from, nor where the Wind of God is going. So, no one understands why the Wind ceases to blow. We can only be thankful that the Wind of God did blow on the Isle of Lewis from 1949-53.

Rev. James Murray MacKay

Rev. Murdo MacLennan

The Barvas Church

Donald Macphail

Christine Smith,
Rev. Duncan Campbell
and Peggy Smith

Chapter nine

"THE REVIVAL OF 1960-1965"

('DUSGADH 1960-1965)

I include this revival on the Isle of Lewis, although there is such a scarcity of material available concerning it. All I have been able to find suggests that the Revival of 1960-1965 was more localized in a few parishes on the island. This spiritual movement did not impact the entire island as the Revivals of 1934-39 and 1949-53 did.

Several things may have had an effect on this revival. Two years after the close of the Lewis Revival of 1949-53, Billy Graham came to Glasgow, Scotland for the "Tell Scotland" campaign. One cannot place the Billy Graham Crusade in the camp of revival. It was an evangelistic campaign, wonderful, glowing, and God-honoring, but not in the tradition of great revival where the glory of God comes down.

The Billy Graham "Tell Scotland" Crusade was a six weeks campaign during March and April, 1955. During those six weeks in Kelvin Hall in Glasgow, there were 26,457 inquirers concerning salvation in Jesus Christ.(1)

Another revival that may have had an influence on the Lewis Revival of 1960-1965 occurred on the Island of North Uist. North Uist is one of the Hebrides Islands lying just south of the Isle of Lewis and Harris. This is an island of heather and moorland. Few trees trim the landscape. It is an island of lochs, an island of water, water and water. John Ferguson says concerning North Uist, "The multi-colored riot of wild flowers on the fertile machair (or grass-land by the sea), corn marigolds, poppies, bugle, eyebright, silverweed, birdsfoot-trefoil, buttercups, and orchids, and the mystic ever-present vistas of the sea, combine to make it one of the most beautiful places on earth." (2)

The Island of North Uist is populated by villages with names like Lochmaddy, Tigharry, Bayhead, Grimsay, Sollas, and Carinish. It was to this island that great revival came in

1957-58.

The revival that came to North Uist in 1957-58 came under the ministry of four young lady Pilgrims who were with the Faith Mission. Jean Wilson and Margaret Macintyre from North Ireland, Daphne Parker from Leicestershire, and Mary Morrison who was from the village of Ness on the Isle of Lewis. Interestingly, Mary Morrison had been converted to Christ under the preaching of Duncan Campbell in the Lewis Revival of 1949-53.

The early 1960's seem to have ushered in a sprinkling of the Holy Spirit in England and Scotland. It seemed as if the Lord was wanting to do a great work in the United Kingdom.

I have in my library a letter I received from a Baptist Pastor friend of mine in England. He wrote to share what God had done in his life in 1966. I think you will enjoy his personal experience with the Lord.

"On a Saturday afternoon in Ribchester, Lancs, I was out in the back garden, nipping off the heads of broad bean plants to protect them from blackfly. The next day I was to preach on the subject of the Pharisee and the Publican, and, as I nipped off the heads of a plant, I heard a voice within say, You are the Pharisee!' This rebuke came with such force that I felt I must go inside the house and I felt driven to pray. Soon tears of repentance were flowing and I felt a presence in the back bedroom where I had gone to pray. It was though a very bright light was shining in the room, but I am sure it was a light within my soul rather than without in the room. I also felt like I was glowing, and I remember calling on God as I looked up to the corner of the ceiling.

This went on for some time, I think a few hours, and I eventually began to think that I must leave the room and prepare for Liz returning home from shopping. As I went to open the door, a fear gripped me that the presence' would fly out of the room, and I would return to normality. I did, however, open the door and felt like I was filled with God's presence.

The effect on me was that I found prayer and communion with God not only a delight, but so very easy. I found myself rising at dawn (which is quite early in July), and seeing the sun rise in the east from our small, front bedroom window. I had decided to make that room my meeting place with God, and for twelve weeks I lived in ecstasy and blessing. Somehow sin and temptation did not trouble me. I had boundless energy and longed simply to pray and read God's Word. It was absolutely thrilling, exciting and energizing. I could not get enough of God's presence. To this day, I do not know whether anyone noticed a change in me, but I did. Some evidence of my Bible study can be found in the large AV Bible I hold in my study. My notes in Matthew 1-5 were written in the margins during this period. The study of the genealogy of Christ was particularly thrilling to me at that time.

After twelve weeks, we had to go to Liz's farm in Dolphinholme, something I was reluctant to do due to this sudden blessing. I had a fear of losing my new routine and leaving my room of prayer. However, we had to go, and I decided that I would rise at dawn and continue to pray. I awoke on the first morning, and felt back to normal, the presence which had gripped me had gone. However, I imagined that it was because I had left my room and routine and felt that when I returned it would be OK. When we did return, I could not recapture God's presence and felt rather flat. This was a great sadness, and yet, many years later I know that something happened, and if I had a foretaste of heaven's glory, then eternity will be absolutely wonderful.

Some years later, I recounted this experience to Rev. Crawford MacIntyre who asked, What did the experience do for you?' I knew it had thrilled me, lifted me into realms of blessing, but I had never even considered his question. On reflection, I feel it gave me a great assurance of salvation, and the reality of God in my life, and increased my faith in Him.

Sadly, most of the sins and trials I regret have occurred since that time, so I know for sure that what happened did not leave me entirely sanctified. Like the face of Moses, the glow faded and that is indeed a sadness simply because I know I have tasted something of the presence of God. I also learned that one cannot rely on experience(s), but on the solid truth and facts of Scripture. I have been reluctant to speak about this because of the reasons mentioned earlier, and also because I actually lost the blessing in the sense of its glory and energizing power.

Some will wonder whether like Hannah in I Samuel, I had been at the drink and like Eli, say, How long wilt thou be drunken?' But, like Hannah, I know I was not drunk. I have never been drunk, or even felt nearly drunk. What happened to me simply happened. I was not seeking it, and I was surprised by it. All I know is that it happened suddenly, and ended as quickly as it came. I know it was not a fantasy, and try as I might, I cannot re-create the blessing.

Just as today, Friday, the 9th of January, 2004, I struggle with the mysteries of providence. In my duties as Pastor of SBC, this very week I have a dear Christian sister who seems to be dying of cancer. Yesterday I was in the home of a lady whose son was found dead in his bedroom. He had lovingly cared for his housebound mother who was felt to be dying three years ago. Her husband and I arranged her funeral while I was in the USA, but he died before her, and now her caring son, who has just recovered from severe alcoholism has been suddenly taken.

Added to that, a recent convert in his 60's was rushed to St. Thomas's Hospital in London with a chronic angina attack. In simple faith he asked for prayer and the doctors now cannot find anything wrong with him. They are mightily puzzled, but he is confessing to all and sundry that the Lord has healed him. We have seen several miracles happen to this man, not least his amazing conversion, and that of his partner (now spouse after conviction concerning their relationship).

On my morning walks, I often see him, and this once unbeliever asks me for prayer and sometimes we pray together in his barn, fields or in the farmyard. I record this to highlight that some things happen which I cannot explain, others question and deny, but I know what I see and have seen. Some of it has proved to be wheat, some chaff, but God is still at work despite all the bad things we see in our country and in our time." (3)

As the sprinklings of the glory threw themselves here and there in England and Scotland during this period of time, revival came once again to the Isle of Lewis. The Revival of 1960-1965 in Lewis did not grip the entire island as some of the previous revivals had done. The Revival of 1960-65 was more localized to a few parishes.

Revival came to the village of Callanish. At this time, the congregation at Callanish was a part of the congregation of Carloway. It was the church in Carloway that had seen such glorious times in the Revival of 1934-39 , and then again in 1949-53. In the congregation at Callanish in 1960-1965, the revival seemed to focus on married couples when quite a number of them came to the Lord.

In 1960-65, there was a similar movement of God in the

church at Back and at Knock. It was during the Knock revival that the Rev. Neil Shaw was converted to Christ. Shaw eventually became the minister at Dingwall. (4)

The present minister of the Free Church in Back on the Isle of Lewis is Rev. Iain D. Campbell. Campbell said, "In Callanish and Back, in the late 1960's and 1970's, many young couples were converted and became member of Christ's church. Many of these young men are now elders in the church, and others have become preachers of the Gospel. Similar movements among young people in Point and in Stornoway took place, resulting in an increased vitality within the churches. An almost universal feature of these revivals was the marked contrast between the old and the new in the lifestyle of those who were born again. Old habits, places, interests, all gave way to the coming of truth into the life. This must always be the evidence of true conversion, and is certainly the evidence of true revival." (5)

One wonders if this revival that came to Lewis in 1960-65 was influenced by the great outpouring of the Spirit of the Lord on Lewis in 1949-53. Could it have been a continuation of that revival? Could there have been a pause in the heavenly breath, and then, God came down again.

One also wonders if this 1960-1965 revival could have been a result of the heightened spiritual sensitivity brought on by the Billy Graham "Tell Scotland A Crusade of 1955.

We don't know the answers to those questions. We will never know. We can only step in, take a look, and say, "God did it."

Chapter ten

"THE REVIVAL OF 1969-1973"

('DUSGADH 1969-1973)

The revival that came to Lewis in 1969-73 was not one that covered the whole island as previous revivals had done. The revival of 1969-73 was localized in two areas; the Free Church of Stornoway, and the small village of Lemraway.

LEMRAWAY

If you leave the town of Stornoway, and head south on Highway A859.for about sixteen miles , you come to Highway B8060 which turns to the left. If you follow that road for twelve miles, you come to the tiny fishing village of Lemraway. This village is tucked neatly along the east coast of the Isle of Lewis. The road leading to Lemraway is a dead-end road. The village is isolated and compact.

The Revival of 1949-53 had its beginning in December, 1949. The next year, 1950, Duncan Campbell, the Highland preacher of the revival, had a strong, urgent desire to go to the village of Lemraway to preach. Because of strong opposition, he was prevented from going.

During the great Lewis Revival of 1949-53, Duncan Campbell went to the Island of Bernera to preach in 1951. During his time on Bernera, a young man by the name of Donald Macaulay was converted to Christ.

Donald Macaulay had served in the national military. When he returned home from his service to his country, he signed as a boat crewman, and traveled for eighteen months in South America and the United States. When he returned home to Bernera, people were talking about the revival. Macaulay was encouraged by his family and his friends to attend the revival services. During the time Duncan Campbell was on the island, Donald Macaulay was converted to Christ.

In 1969, this same man, Donald Macaulay, was the

minister of the Church of Scotland in the village of Lamraway. He invited Duncan Campbell to come and preach at the Communion Services in Lemraway. Campbell felt immediately that the church was very close to revival. Suddenly, wonderfully, the fire of God fell on the church in Lemraway. How strange that Duncan Campbell had had a passion to come to this church twenty years earlier, but was unable to. Now, twenty years later he comes to preach, and the Spirit of God pours out on the people.

Donald Macaulay said concerning this revival, "When the revival broke out, the presence of the Lord was felt all around Lemraway. It seemed to be a circle around the village, or a canopy over the area. Outside of this circle there was nothing; it was just so ordinary.....It did not last very long, nor did it spread any further than Lemraway." (1)

It is mysterious, indeed, that the power of God never left Duncan Campbell. He preached in the power of the Holy Spirit until his death in 1972. One can truly say that the unction of the Lord was upon him. I am sure that the revival in Lemraway in 1969 reminded Duncan Campbell of his time on Lewis from 1949-53. It was Barvas all over again.

Donald Macaulay, the Lemraway minister, said, "We had services in the church every night at 6:00 p.m. Nobody wanted to leave. We would go to the nearby manse, have a cup of tea, and then return to the pulpit for another hour-and-a-half. The people still would not go home, but gathered in the manse for yet more preaching, singing and fellowship. People left the manse for work in the morning before they went home." (2)

STORNOWAY

The town of Stornoway is the largest town on the Isle of Lewis. In 1970, it had a population of perhaps 11,000 people.

To a large degree, the Revival of 1934-39, and the Revival of 1949-53 bypassed Stornoway. There was no great, mighty outpouring of the Holy Spirit in Stornoway during these times. The reason could have been the severe opposition to the revivals by the minister of the Free Church of Stornoway, Rev. Kenneth Macrae.

Rev. Macrae came to the Free Church of Stornoway in the 1930s. He was a great preacher of the gospel. He was deeply loved, and admired , not only by his church, but by the entire Free Church denomination. When revival broke out on Lewis in the 1930s, and again in 1949, Rev. Macrae was bitterly opposed to it for three reasons; he opposed the physical manifestations of the revivals, he was opposed to the doctrine of the fullness of the Holy Spirit which Duncan Campbell preached, and he accused Duncan Campbell of not being Calvinist in his belief. The churches on the Isle of Lewis are strictly Calvinistic in their belief.

In 1965, Rev. Kenneth Macrae died, and the Free Church had the task of finding someone to take his place. It was not an easy assignment, because of the long tenure of Macrae, and the deep attachment the people had for him.

We should remember that the Free Church in Stornoway is the largest church in all of Scotland. It has been that for many, many years. It is quite common for 1200-1500 people to crowd the church on Sunday night. For generations, this church has stood as the beacon of the gospel of Jesus Christ, not only to Scotland, but to the entire United Kingdom.

In 1966, the Free Church in Stornoway called Rev. Murdo Macritchie to be its minister. Macritchie was born in Back, Lewis in 1920. When he was a teen-ager, he became deeply aware of his need of a Savior from listening to the preaching of Rev. Murdoch Macrae of Kinloch. He was converted to Christ, and began his long walk with the Lord. It is interesting to note that Murdo Macritchie was converted to Christ during the time when God was walking across the Isle of Lewis in great power during the revival of 1934-39.

When World War II broke out, Murdo Macritchie did as many of the Lewis young men did, he joined the Royal Navy. He served at Dunkirk and in the North Atlantic during the war, but, in 1942, he was discharged due to bad health. During his time in the Navy, Macritchie became aware of the call of God on his life to be a minister. He entered Edinburgh University, where he won a scholarship to the Westminster Theological Seminary in Philadelphia, Pennsylvania. After completing a degree at the seminary, he was called to be minister of the Free Church in Detroit, Michigan in 1952. He played a leading role in helping to build a church building at this church. He served as minister of the church in Detroit for fifteen years.

In 1966, Macritchie received a call from the Free Church in Stornoway on the Isle of Lewis to replace the renowned Rev. Kenneth Macrae. He faced an awesome task of becoming the minister of the largest church in Scotland, and also trying to replace a man of Rev. Macrae's stature.

Rev. Macritchie had a special gift of relating to young people. During his years at the Free Church of Stornoway, the young, as well as the old, were brought into the spiritual life of the church.

"The young of the congregation were always his main concern though he could equal any in leading the more mature into the riches of Christian truth and experience. But, without doubt, the most important part of his work in Stornoway was the way he brought the young people of the congregation into very close contact with the church; so much so that it is a rare inspiration to preach the gospel on Sabbath evening in the Stornoway church packed with a young and attentive audience. Many of the young people were turned to the Lord during his ministry there and he gained for himself a very special place in their affection." (3)

In 1982, Rev. Macritchie's health began to decline. "In July, 1982, he had to have a leg amputated. He spent some time in the hospital in Edinburgh. On March 10, 1983, he returned to Stornoway, and was finally allowed to return to his home on March 10th. He passed away on April 2, 1983." (4)

Rev. Murdo Macritchie saw revival come to his church in Stornoway from 1971-73. It was a glory time in the church, with many young people coming to know Christ as Savior and Lord of their lives.

God always knows where He is going to work, and He knows why He is working in a particular place. I found it interesting that during this period of revival from 1969-73, God poured out His power and glory in the largest church in Scotland, but He also poured out his grace in Lemraway, one of the most isolated, out-of-the-way places in the world. God works in the large and the small, in the weak and in the mighty.

The Free Church of Scotland ministers on the Isle of Lewis have traditionally been strict Calvinist in their doctrine. They have preached with eloquence and passion the doctrines of predestination and election. These doctrines are ingrained in their very fiber. For some, who are not Calvinist in their belief, these strict beliefs in extreme Calvinism may seem strong, and, sometimes non-evangelistic. Because of their deep- felt belief in the doctrine of Calvinism, the preachers on the Isle of Lewis never give a public invitation. They are afraid they will be interfering with the work of the

Holy Spirit.

I have listened, on tape, to the preaching of Rev. Murdo Macritchie. I have never heard a more urgent cry to the lost. He preached with a heartfelt passion for the lost. He implored people to come to Christ. It is preaching at its very best, as he invites men, women and young people to accept Christ as Savior and Lord of their lives.

Those of you who are reading this book need to hear Rev. Murdo Macritchie. I only wish you could listen to him preach, but the next best thing is to read his preaching as he pours out his heart concerning the story of the rich, young ruler. His text is Mark 10:17-22. As you read these words, listen to them with your heart, and with your soul.

"THE RICH, YOUNG RULER"

Mark 10:17-22

This is the narrative of the rich, young ruler. We learn from Matthew that he was a young man. We learn from Luke that he was a ruler. All three gospels tell us he was a rich man.

He came running to Jesus. He came with haste. He wanted to attend to it immediately. He would have been an excellent business man. He didn't succeed in business by leaving things lying until the next day. We find him here running to Jesus. This speaks of something better to come. This person is interested in spiritual matters. On one hand, we have to be thoughtful, on the other hand, we have to be cautious. There are many instances in the Bible of people being interested in religious matters for a little time, then they appear to leave off such matters, and even turn their backs on it.

This man came running to Jesus. He didn't appear

haughty or arrogant. He wasn't self-confident or reckless. He came to Jesus and kneeled before him, and asked, "Good Master, what must I do that I might inherit eternal life?"

Having riches, he wanted to add something to it. He probably understood that there was a life hereafter. He realized there was an area where he was not settled, the area of the life hereafter. If there was an eternal life, he wanted to know what he could do to inherit it.

He said, "Good Master" and knelt before Him. It was a posture of reverence. The Lord didn't find any fault in him for kneeling before Him. Our Lord sees the heart. He understands the ignorance of the human heart. He understands the darkness of the mind. He realizes how people have been captivated and captured by the power of darkness.

This is very unlike what we ourselves think. If the question were asked of you or me, some of us would say that we will just let it pass for now, seeing it might hinder our religious progress.

The Lord was of a different opinion. He said, "Why do you call me good?" It doesn't mean he wasn't good. We shall see that this man did not appreciate Him as the Son of God.

Jesus knew very well that this young man didn't understand that He was the Savior of the lost. He considered Him as a man only, who was doing wonderful works. We see the same thing with Nicodemus, who came and began complimenting Jesus on His good works.

I think it would do us all good to go through the New Testament and consider the people who came to Jesus. He seems to be putting them off, rather than asking them to come.

The Syro-Phoenician woman who comes to Him. Jesus said he was only sent to the lost sheep of the house of Israel. It was not proper for the children's food to be thrown to the dogs.

The man who came with his child after the Lord had been on the Mt. Of Transfiguration, and he said, "If you can, help us." Jesus said, "If you can, believe."

We find the same thing with the woman of Samaria at the well. She thought she had escaped detection when the Lord pulls his sword and plunges it into her soul, and says, "I know you have no husband." He reveals to her her past life.

Why do you think the Lord did these things? One thing we do know, He always did the right thing. That doesn't answer the question I have asked. Why? One possible answer I would offer is this, when a person is made a new creation in Christ, he has to be demolished. It is not a repair work. The thing has to be turned inside out. It is human nature for us to think that, as a people, we are not too bad. Therefore, all I need is a bit of repair, some restoration, so that we can make eternal life. That is the view that is next to the heart of each one of us as sinners.

The Roman Church idea of faith is that there is an ocean to be crossed and with your own small boat you can cross quite a ways, but you can't make it to the other side, so you ask for help so that God will take you on board a bigger ship in order to cross to the other side. That is not the teaching of Scripture, but it is a teaching that is very attractive to the unregenerate heart. It fits in well with the way a sinner thinks.

This man was a religious man. There are religious men and women in our congregation who do not know the Lord Jesus Christ. People of fine character. People you would trust with anything. You would give them a reference at work, wholeheartedly, knowing they would not let you down. But, friends, that is not being a new creation in Christ Jesus. Far from it!

"Why do you call me good?" Jesus as much as says, "Do you realize what you are saying? I am good, but not because you are calling me good. There is no one good but God."

I don't know what your doctrine of God is, but I know that my doctrine of God comes tremendously short of the doctrine of God set forth in His Word. We play around with the Word, play around with the concept. Our concept of God becomes something that we manufacture, something we can handle. As long as you can handle a god, you can do anything with it. If you create a god, you can do anything with him. Plato spoke of a supreme good. Oh! That is a god, but not the God of the Bible. That is a god of my mind, my imagination, my understanding, and I can work it, mold it, handle that god. How different is that to God, the Creator, the Judge in whose hands everything is.

You remember the king of old as he drank out of the vessels of the temple. He was reminded that he did not honor the God in whose hands his very breath was. If you realize that the breath you breathe, the power of your muscles, the motion of your mind is in the hand of God. It is a frightening thought, on one hand, but to those who have found peace with God in Christ, it is a most comforting thought. Come what may, from every side, you know that God is there, and that God is there on your behalf.

The young man had no thought that he wouldn't be able to inherit eternal life. So, the Lord tells him about the commandments. You notice where the Lord takes him, to the second table of the law. He told him plainly. The second table of the law is man's relationship with man. The first table of the law deals with man's relationship with God. He tells him, "Do not commit adultery, do not kill, do not steal, do not be a false witness, do not fraud, honor your father and mother. These were things the man would be able to know if he were doing or not.

But, the answer the man gave showed very clearly that he

lacked the spiritual perception necessary to understand the very deep requirements of God's law. Outward performance for obedience is not true under the old law or the new.

I'm not saying performance was not honored by God. It says the Lord loved this man, and it had something to do with the performance of his outward life, but, friends, however a person is in his character, it is not sufficient for salvation.

The young man says, "All these things I have done from my youth." The man honestly answered that he had kept them all. The Lord then gives him another means of testing. He says, "One thing you lack, sell whatever you have." The Lord answered in such a different way than the young man anticipated.

Has the Lord brought you to a knowledge of your sins, and a knowledge of Himself in exactly the way you thought it would happen? It doesn't seem to be that way in the New Testament, nor the Old. The Lord does things in His own way, not in yours, not in mine.

The Lord brings about a change in the whole conversation. He brings up something entirely new. The man could have said, "I came to you with a simple question. How could I inherit eternal life? That was all I was concerned about. Now this man is asking me to sell everything I have. What does this have to do with my property, my riches, my inheritance?"

The Lord saw that this man was going to add it as an extension to his own unregenerate self. That can't be done. You can't attach eternal life to an unregenerate person. NO!

There may be many here tonight who would like eternal life, but you would like it on your own terms. I can tell you this, if you ever get eternal life, you will never get it on your terms. It is you who has to come to terms with God. The terms of God are clear. The terms of God are unconditional. If God be as willing to receive me as I am to receive Him, then there will be no delay. Wait a minute! Are you sure you are not saying this, "If Christ be willing to receive me on my terms, I will come." Well, He never will! You have to receive Him on His terms, his terms alone.

The young man said, "I came with a simple question. This person delves into my private affairs, my riches. What does eternal life have to do with that?"

The Lord sees the sore spot. He doesn't say, "I'd better not offend him by mentioning his riches." The Lord could see that his riches had encased his heart, that this was the greatest single obstacle, that he was obsessed with riches. He wanted riches, along with eternal life.

So, the Lord places His finger on the very sore point, and he presses it. He will not yield at all to this man. He wants this man to yield to Him.

When the Lord presses a finger on a sore spot in your experience, in your heart, in your life, something hidden that no one knows, and that is what is keeping you away, you know you have to give it up. You have to abandon it. You know you have to bid farewell to whatever it is. No one knows it, but you know it. Remember, we cannot serve two masters. The Lord is a jealous God. He is extremely jealous. You can't give your heart to another and give your heart to Christ as well.

This man is perplexed. He doesn't know what to do. He wishes he had never gone to the market that day. He came that day to inherit eternal life. Undoubtedly he had some money on him.

It would be wonderful tonight if you would discover that you cannot win eternal life by the life you live. I'm not saying you shouldn't pray, come to church, read your Bible. We should do all this. If you come out of your house one day, and say, "I have received eternal life. I have worked hard at this. I have worked incessantly at this. I have read about it in many, many books. I have found just the way to do it. I have managed it at last." What a great accomplishment that would be for you. NO, friend! You are outside. There is no place for you in the choir that sings the praises of the redeemed. For those who sing his praises will give all the glory to Him. They will throw their crowns at His feet. It is to Him, and to Him alone.

So, this man hears the Lord say, "One thing you lack." You can almost hear him say, "Well, if it's only one thing, surely I can get away with that, if it is only one thing."

The Lord goes on, "Go your way, sell whatever you have." You can almost hear the young man thinking, There are two balances before his eyes. The scales are before his eyes. On one hand, there is eternal life on the scales. On the other scale there are his possessions. What will he do? If it worth it? All my possessions? I wouldn't mind being a great giver, giving my money away and seeing what it would do for people. But, give it all away? That means I would be a pauper. I would have nothing left.

Friend, is there anything in your life that is keeping you from the Lord. There are things that are instrumental in driving people further and further away from Christ, and acting as barriers in keeping them from thinking seriously about their souls, because they are so obsessed by them that they cannot bear to think of even abandoning them at all.

But, they want to come with all that, and the Lord says, "No! You can't! Your heart is not right. You are set on earthly things and you want the treasures of heaven."

Do you realize what eternal life means? There has to be a demolition. There has to be a breaking down. Oh, Yes! No one has ever received Christ as Savior without being broken down, broken down in your soul.

Nothing gives more delight than the person you have known for years, and is quite proud and self-confident. Then you meet that person after the Lord has dealt graciously with his soul. He is so different. He has been broken.

Has the Lord broken your self-confidence? Has the Lord broken your soul? Has He? It is a delight. A person says, "Well, I'm saved." That doesn't mean anything. It doesn't necessarily mean what is said. If the only way your salvation can be known is by your saying, "I'm saved", then something is lacking.

You can always see the scales, back and forth, back and forth. It is a tug-of-war.

This rich, young ruler doesn't find any words. The Lord has given him a test. And, the young man can administer the test himself. The Lord doesn't have to come around to see if he has cheated. The man applies the test. What does he do? He goes away, and he was very sad."Sell all you have, give it to the poor, and come follow me." The cross was too heavy for him.

You are here, very young, you would like to be a Christian, but what would your friends say? What would your husband say if you went after Christ? What would your wife think of you? What would your children think?

Oh, you are a respectable church-goer, but you are not a member. You are not involved. These things will not go on forever. This man went away sad. Why? Because he had great possessions. You may only have a small percentage of what that man had, but you have one thing that man had. You have the possession of self-righteousness. But, you are saying tonight, "I'm not self-righteous. I'm just an ordinary person."

Are you sure you are not self-righteous? There is a test for self-righteousness. Here it is! Bring your heart into confrontation with the cross of Calvary, with the work of the Lord Jesus Christ, and see how it responds. Take your heart to the place where Christ saves.

You see, God has to convince you of your sinnership. It doesn't mean you have to cry out, or have a one or two hour crisis. No! The Lord works in mysterious ways to convince people of their sinnership.

There are many indications. You see a change coming over their heart, their desires for the gospel. Now, the children of God may try to hasten them. That is a very dangerous thing. Have you ever seen eggs about to be hatched? You would expect the chickens to be hatched today. But, they are not. Children sometimes will break the shell too soon, and kill the chicken.

Oh, the desire to see one come out of the shell, to push too much. We have to entreat , to encourage, to warn, to appeal for people to come out of the grave, out of the shell, but it is only the Lord that can do it.

The wonderful doctrine of predestination, which is so clearly set forth in God's Word, has been used by our own people as a means of destruction of their own soul and souls of others. They say, "I can't do anything." You know this, when a person is convinced he is a sinner, and that he needs salvation, he leaves off all this abstract reasoning and does all he can, and in all his breathless activity, he falls down. Then, God lifts him up in His wonderful grace.

This is what God is teaching people all their lives. This evening, I am more concerned with those of you who are still in your sins, still without Christ. If we had left this rich, young man on his deathbed, we might think he was saved, for he was very sad and sorrowful. But, there is no indication he was a changed man, because, along with his sorrow, the basic reason was still hanging around his neck, his possessions.

His sorrow did not save. You must look to the sorrow of another. Will you not turn as you are, in all your sinfulness? Christ is offered to you tonight, in all His fullness.

Especially young boys and girls, don't let your lives pass by. Why will you not give your lives to the Lord Jesus?

In the days of our Lord, the teachers of the law were holding the door fast shut to God. May we ministers of the gospel today not do that.

This will pass by, and some of you will go home with all kinds of sorrows. Others will say, "I've heard that so often. Why don't they preach other things? Why don't preachers just expound the Word, and leave it there. Why do preachers meddle in our personal lives?"

The people of God are entreating you in love. They know, and God knows that you are harboring something that is keeping you away from Christ. (5)

Although the Revival of 1969-73 was not felt across the Isle of Lewis, it was deeply felt in two places; in Lemraway and in Stornoway. Little Lemraway, and Big Stornoway! How wonderful that the God of heaven would come down and visit both of these churches in all of His glory. The Dear Lord used Duncan Campbell in Lemraway, and Murdo Macritchie in Stornoway to preach the wonderful grace of God in Christ Jesus.

Chapter eleven

“THE REVIVAL OF 1984-1987”

(‘DUSGADH 1984-1987)

On the northern end of the Isle of Lewis sits the small village of Ness. It sits among scattered houses, large church buildings, heather, and the dashing waves of the sea, pounding against the rocks of the seashore. On October 15, 1935, a baby boy was born in Ness, who would grow up to have a great spiritual impact, not only on the Isle of Lewis, but on the nation of Scotland. The name given to him was Murdo Alex Macleod.

All his life, he was affectionately called Murdo Alex. He was the son of the Free Church minister in Ness. While growing up, his one main passion in life was football (soccer). He was an exceptional player. He played for the Nicolson Institute team in the 1950s. Matthew Maciver said of Murdo Alex, "The first clear memory I have is of a match against the RAF at Goathill....We won 4-0 that night, and our two stars were Murdo Alex Macleod and Willie John Campbell. They were outstanding and seemed to beat the RAF on their own.....I only once spoke to Murdo Alex in a private capacity. I met him after a Sunday morning service in Edinburgh....I even went so far as to tell him that from the perspective of a ten-year-old boy from Portnaguran, he had chosen the wrong vocation. He should, I said, have become a professional footballer, and not a Minister of the gospel. He laughed and admitted that he had never lost his love for football." (1)

There was always a running joke in the Macleod household. Murdo Alex always said he ran a divided house. He was a life-long fan of the Rangers football team, while one of his sons was an avid Celtic fan. Murdo Alex claimed that son was tolerated in the family.

In 1955, an event happened that changed the course of Macleod's life. He was converted to Christ. He entered Aberdeen University in 1960 to prepare his life for the calling of God into the gospel ministry. During his life, he served four churches. He began his ministry in 1966 in Drumchapel. He went to Dingwall in 1972, to Greyfriars Church in Inverness in 1978, and was called to the Free Church of Stornoway in 1984.

In one of the obituaries written about Murdo Alex, it stated, "Murdo Alex had a warm, bubbling humanity. His impish sense of humor and incorrigible addiction to practical jokes were legendary." (2)

From the very beginning of his ministry, to the end, Murdo Alex believed that the voice of God spoke through the Holy Scriptures with a message of the redemptive love of Jesus Christ. He had one passion, the salvation of the lost.

When he came to the large, Free Church of Stornoway, it was a time of change. Murdo Alex had seen that the church in Scotland had lost much over the years. He had watched a spiritual declension in his nation. He came to Stornoway to preach the everlasting gospel of Jesus Christ. However, during his time in Stornoway, he introduced many changes. He worked hard at making changes in the ministry to young people. The changes he made in the outreach to young people was borne on the wings of his deep love for youth. "The young people of the island were particularly close to his heart, and he never failed to represent them in the best possible light , and to urge those who touched their lives most directly to treat them with compassion and understanding." (3)

In May, 1995, Murdo Alex Macleod was elected as Moderator of the General Assembly of the Free Church of Scotland, an honor bestowed upon him because of the deep love and respect the people of the Free Church had for him.

In October, 1995, Murdo Alex was in Aberdeen, Scotland at the home of one of his sons. He was on his way to Holland for a meeting. On October 15th, the family celebrated his 60th birthday. The next day, Murdo Alex Macleod died suddenly in the home of his son.

The Free Church of Stornoway, as well as the entire Isle of Lewis, was stunned. They agonized in deep grief. The funeral service was scheduled at the Free Church in Stornoway for 2:00 in the afternoon. The church was packed to capacity forty-five minutes before time for the service. By the time the funeral service began, hundreds of people were filling the streets outside the church.

Since the custom of the Free Church is only the singing of the Psalms, the vast congregation sang the 23rd Psalm, "The Lord is my Shepherd." It would have been difficult to find a dry eye in the crowd.

When the funeral was concluded at the church, the long-standing tradition of Lewis was followed by the carrying of the casket to the cemetery. The streets of Stornoway were crowded with people as the procession made its way for a full mile. Men would carry the casket for a few steps. They would then step aside, and other men would take their place. Each man wanted the opportunity to carry their beloved Minister a few steps toward the burial ground. Old men, who could hardly walk, stepped in to take their turn. Young boys dressed in their school uniforms would carry for a few steps.

"He was a typical Highland minister. He was fully assured in his own beliefs, defiantly confident in his church's form of worship, observer of all its taboos and totally paranoid about the press. He was constantly teasing, constantly leg-pulling, and constantly outrageous. Every minister and elder and every venerable matron who attended that service knew they were at the funeral of the bubbliest human being in Scotland. Yet they were overwhelmed with a sense of spiritual loss." (4)

It was this man, Murdo Alex Macleod, who came to the Free Church in Stornoway in 1984. He was replacing the Rev. Murdo Macritchie, who had died in 1983, after 17 years as Minister of the church.

Revival was not long coming to the Free Church, Stornoway, after Murdo Alex Macleod became its Minister. Almost immediately a sense of spiritual awakening began to move through the church. From 1984 to 1987, the church felt the wonderful, refreshing breeze of the Holy Spirit blow through the congregation. Many of those who were converted to Christ during this period were young people. It seems that Murdo Alex had a special gift that related to the youth.

The Free Church in Stornoway will hold 1200 people. It was quite common for the church to be filled to capacity on Sunday morning and Sunday evening. On Sunday evening, a large number of the congregation was made up of young people who had come to hear Murdo Alex tell the wonderful story of salvation through Jesus Christ.

I realize that what is coming next does not do justice to the preaching of Murdo Alex Macleod. To read a sermon on paper will not share the full personality of the preacher. I have listened to Murdo Alex Macleod preach on tape. I only wish I could have heard him in person. Listening to him on tape, one can catch the passion he had for those who were lost from God. You can hear in his voice his deep, abiding love for Jesus Christ. You can note his compassion for the people to whom he preached.

In the typical Free Church worship service on the Isle of Lewis, they will sing Psalms, have prayers, and the minister will preach, then they will close with a Psalm. The following sermon was preached by Murdo Alex Macleod in the Free

Church in Stornoway, on Sunday night, February 27, 1994. His subject was the Gadarene demoniac, recorded in Luke 8:22-39 , and in Mark 5:1-20. When the worship service began that Sunday night, the order of service was:

Song: Psalm 145:1-7
Prayer: Murdo Alex Macleod
Song: Psalm 40:1-5
Scripture reading: Luke 8:22-39
Song: Psalm 107:10-16
Scripture reading: Mark 5:1-20
Sermon: Murdo Alex Macleod
NOW, listen to Murdo Alex Macleod preach!

"This incident is recorded by the three synoptic gospels; Matthew, Mark and Luke. It seems this man confronted Jesus when he stepped ashore in the area belonging to the Gadarenes. The region in which this man was found was limestone caves and rock chambers where dead bodies were buried. This was the kind of place frequented by those who were demon-possessed. It is difficult to establish the mental condition of this man. We have here a case of mental disorder, mental derangement which was made worse by the presence of these evil spirits. He was driven by this mental condition, and by the possession of these demons to frequent, day and night, this area.

It is also difficult to determine when the man's actions, and the man's words were those of his own, or those of the demons. There are times when it seems he is speaking as a man who was mentally deranged, but also demon-possessed. This is one of those difficult times when we are confronted with demon-possession in the gospels.

The New Testament gives us a vivid description of this

man's mental state. Putting all three accounts together, you get a picture of a man who was violent and uncontrollable. There was an absence of self-control in this man's life. He had both homicidal and suicidal tendencies. When he is confronted by Jesus, he goes into one of these frenzies. Here Jesus Christ comes face to face with this kind of influence.

The first thing that happened: The demons challenge the manifestation of this divine presence. "What have I to do with Thee, Jesus, Thou Son of the Most High God?" Whether these are the words of the mentally-deranged man, or the demons, is not clear, but, most likely, it is the estimate of both the man and the demons.

There is a direct challenge to the power and the presence of Jesus. This is nothing new in the Scriptures, in history, nor nothing new for us today. The power and the presence of Jesus are always challenged by the presence of evil. You might very well say that the Bible itself is an account of the conflict between evil and God. It began in the Garden of Eden when Adam and Eve were challenged by Satan as to the authority of God. It continued in the history of Israel and Egypt where Pharaoh challenged the power and authority of God manifested through Moses. It occurred at the time of Elijah and Ahab. Ahab was the representative of evil and Elijah the representative of God. The presence of God was challenged by the power of evil. When Jesus was born, Herod represented the presence and power of evil, challenging the account of the birth of Jesus. Herod tried to rid the world of Jesus by putting to death as many new-born baby boys as he could.

It was by the death of Jesus on the cross that evil, principalities and powers, were triumphed over. And yet, after his resurrection and ascension, when he had commissioned His apostles to preach the gospel, they were always confronted by evil. In the Book of Acts, time and time again, evil was represented in the lives of individuals who tried to destroy the apostles, destroy the gospel, discredit the gospel.

And, there is the same in the world today. Wherever Christ and the gospel confront evil, evil will always go into a frenzy, trying everything to destroy and discredit the gospel of Christ, and the Christ of the gospel.

This is one instance where you see the wrath of the devil and the frenzy of evil being expressed in the presence of Jesus. When Jesus confronts this man, he goes into one of these frenzies that, from time to time, we have an account of in the New Testament. Remember the distraught father who came with his boy? The same thing happened before Jesus cast the devils out of him.

One of the reasons why evil finds expression like this is because the presence of Jesus constrains evil.

"What have I to do with Thee?" said the demons to Jesus. It is as if they are saying they would rather have the gulf that exists between them and Christ left as it is. Whenever Jesus comes into that area, the devils are constrained to acknowledge, not only their own existence and their presence, but also to acknowledge the power of Christ. They recognize, with fear, that here is One who can control them, even as they try to control others.

You see how this is expressed in the life of an individual today. When a man, woman, boy or girl is converted to Christ, whenever grace takes up abode in the heart of an individual, it is immediately confronted by evil, by darkness and sin. Sin cannot abide the presence of grace in Christ. That is what causes the conflict. They are locked in conflict.

Paul knew that conflict, and crying out in the midst of that conflict, said, "O, wretched man that I am! Who shall deliver me from this body of death?" That is always the case, because grace exposes sin. Light exposes darkness. Darkness is made to acknowledge its own presence.

Such is the madness of Satan, that though he knows that God and life and grace are far more powerful and effective than himself, he is still bent on destroying it, and extinguishing the light.

Some of you here tonight who are Christians may know that part of the difficulty in living the Christian life. You know there is present with you and always accompanying you, one who wants to destroy you. The devil only disturbs those who are in Christ, or who are in the process of being brought to Christ.

Tonight, I want to speak of this man's request to stay with Jesus, but Jesus told him, "No, you go home to your family, and tell what great things the Lord has done for you."

I want to bring up one or two other things in this story. One thing I have to avoid, because I have got difficulty with it: demon-possession. I am not too sure what it is. As far as I know, I have never come in contact with it. I know people who claim they have met people who were demon-possessed. Be that as it may be, it is certain there were cases of it in the lifetime of our Lord.

Not only did these demons recognize the presence, power, and authority of Jesus, but they knew that he was going to touch them. They knew things would never be the same again, once He came.

So, they made this strange two-fold request: Don't send us out of this country, and don't send us into the deep, into the lake. The Bible says that Jesus did not refuse this request.

Remember where this took place, a very narrow shoreline on the Sea of Galilee. On the cliff top was a herd of pigs.

There came this two-fold request. Mark says, "Jesus suffered them." He suffered them to go into the swine.

The demons went out of the man, and made their entry into the pigs. The herd did, then, panic, ran over the cliff, and drowned in the sea.

How do you explain it? Well, I can't. But, I know people who will tell you they have seen people terrorized by the presence of evil. Here, the presence of evil caused panic in animals.

If I were you, I wouldn't laugh at this. I know there are people who would laugh when they hear this. There are people here tonight, even strong men, who feel uncomfortable in the presence of something you do not understand.

There were eyewitnesses there, shepherds who were looking after the pigs. They saw what happened to the pigs, ran off into the town, and related what they saw. The people came, and they addressed a prayer to Jesus. They besought Him to depart out of their land. "Get out! We don't want you here." Here you have people filled with fear, because the presence of Jesus has created something that has upset them. They had lost their herd.

Here is a man who had terrorized the town, and now he is sitting, clothed and in his right mind, at the feet of Jesus. The people had never seen the likes of this.

How did they react? They didn't want Him in their midst. Perhaps they felt the person of Jesus was an intrusion on their peace and tranquility. But, He also had disturbed their lifestyle.

Remember what the demons said to Him, "What have we to do with Thee?" This is something similar to that. "Get out of here!"

This was a prayer which Jesus granted. He left them.

They asked Him to go, and He left them. Do you find this somewhat solemn? That there are people, because of something they have in connection with the gospel of Christ and the church, are afraid of what it might bring into their own lives. These people didn't dispute what had happened to the man, or what had happened to the pigs, but they wanted no more of this. They had had enough of Jesus in their lives.

There are people who look at salvation like that. They are afraid of it, and they don't want it. It's too upsetting. They had rather be left the way they are. "Depart from our midst."

Some of you may think this is a very strange prayer, but I often wonder how many people listen to the gospel, and pray this prayer?

You have heard many people say, "I asked Jesus to come into my life." But, I wonder if a corresponding number of people might say, "I asked Jesus NOT to come into my life?"

May you be here tonight, afraid that might happen to you? Do you know what it is to be afraid of conversion, afraid of Christ?

I wouldn't be surprised if there is not someone here tonight who , because of these very things, would pray this very prayer. As a matter of fact, is praying this prayer right now.

I would leave you with this thought. What, my friend, if Jesus grants your request? What if He goes, never again to come back? It's an awful request to make, but they made it.

What of this healed demoniac? He is sitting, restored to a right relationship to the Lord Jesus Christ, and his fellow human beings. It's a wonderful sight. This poor man, who had been estranged, and people were afraid of him. There are people like that in the world, locked up, a danger to themselves, and a danger to society. This man was like that, but he comes in contact with the power of Christ, and is restored spiritually, his mind whole, and set at liberty, and his relationships are restored. This is a change that Christ brings to any individual. He brings His own peace, His own blessedness, His own happiness, His own contentment. Satisfaction with Christ replaces the misery that leaves men as slaves to sin, and in the grip of the power of evil and of Satan.

It is the same history in the life of every single convert to Christ, the same story to tell, the same testimony to relate, the same witness to bear, that Christ has changed his life.

As a changed man, he makes this request to Jesus, "Lord, let me continue with you." Jesus refuses the request and says, "No! You go back to your own home, your own friends. Tell them what great things the Lord has done for you." He went back home, told them, and they were amazed at his story.

This request by this man is the third prayer we have in this story. First, the prayer of the demons; don't put us out of this country, and don't put us into the deep. Second, the prayer of the Gadarenes; get out of this country. Third, the prayer of this man, let me continue in your presence.

It is perfectly understandable that the man should ask this, because anyone who has come into contact with Jesus wants to be with Jesus. Anyone who has discovered the blessing that He brings into your life is afraid of losing that blessing. Maybe this is the way the man's mind was working. He wanted to stay in the company of Jesus. He was afraid of losing fellowship with Christ. He was afraid of returning to the old scenes. He didn't want to stay any longer in this place where he spent his time, day and night.

Maybe he was afraid of being left to himself. Who knows? Maybe he was afraid of the return of the demons into his own life. "If I am with you, I'll be safe."

He was also afraid of returning to those who had rejected

Christ. Think of where he was going back, people who wanted nothing to do with Jesus. "Lord, can I stay with you from now on?"

You look in the Bible and you find a very important man who thought the same way. Peter, on the Mt. Of Transfiguration, had one of the most wonderful experiences any man has had on earth. "Lord, this is so wonderful. I don't want to leave this place. Let us stay here."

Perhaps you know what it is like to be blessed under the preaching of the gospel, and you want to stay there. If you are enjoying something, you want to stay there. People in fellowship, in prayer, in times of great spiritual movement want things to continue the way they are.

But, it can also be very wrong. Jesus says, "No! You can't go with me. Go home to your friends, and tell them what great things the Lord has done for you."

Jesus had a higher service for him to be engaged in. There was a higher hand behind this man's life. You know how the Old Testament puts it, "Our thoughts are not His thoughts, and our ways are not His ways." How thankful we should be tonight that that is the case, that God knows better than anyone of us. You may want to do a particular thing, even in the name of the Lord, but the Lord won't allow it, because He has something better for you to do. It is not the way you see it, but the way He sees it. So, on the Mt. of Transfiguration, Jesus said to Peter, "Peter, never you mind. You follow me."

The Lord appoints to us our discipline and our work. He comes to us and says, "This will be your life's work. You've got to go tell what great things the Lord has done for you."

Here is Jesus, leaving the country of the Gadarenes. "Get out!" He was told, and He was leaving. But, He was leaving a witness to Himself in their midst, and the witness was this man in whose life the Lord had done great things.

"Go home to your friends and tell them." The application I want to make of this is the fact that conversion does not break your relationship at home, in the community, at work, or in school.

There are some people who think of conversion to Christ as, "Oh, the convert must never again have contact with those with whom he was brought up, and with those he previously rubbed shoulders."

Every convert, every believer has a story to relate. It is first, a personal story. "Tell them what the Lord has done for YOU. Last week-end, sixteen people sat here for the first time at the Lord's Table. Another ten joined the congregation by certificate. It was noised abroad that twenty-six people had associated themselves with the congregation of the Free Church in Stornoway. That is something for which we are profoundly thankful. No doubt, we have been telling other people about that.

But, what did we have to tell them about ourselves? Do you have a personal story, a personal experience with Christ in your life? Are you able to tell what the Lord has done for you. You read stories of conversions, and you tell people about them. And, that is wonderful. But, there is something more wonderful, being able to tell people how you yourself were converted. There is no more interesting story than the one a person can tell about himself.

The Rhyme of the Ancient Mariner derives much of its interest because the man who told it was, himself, the mariner. "You go home and tell your friends what the Lord has done for you."

Can you picture it? He goes home. He speaks of himself in the past, as a man abandoned by society, but the Lord found him in his lostness, heard his cry, and had mercy on him.

It was this man who asked, "What have I to do with Thee?" The Lord told him what he had to do with Him. He was able to tell that he had been delivered from the bondage of sin, that he had been arrested by the power of Christ on the downward path to hell. He had a story to tell. Every convert has a story to tell. The question is, "Have you got one to tell?"

The second point is this, go home and tell what great things the LORD has done for you. The emphasis is on what the LORD has done. Jesus told the man to emphasize what HE had done. Don't spend too much time telling what you were. People know what you were, but they don't know who did it for you. Tell them who did it. The emphasis is on the grace of God.

What is grace? We don't deserve any good thing from Him. Twas grace that taught my heart to fear; twas grace that made my eyes oer'flow. We ascribe it all to the grace of God. This is the song that reverberates through the courts of heaven, grace, grace, glory be to the grace of God.

Thirdly, tell them what GREAT things the Lord has done for you. If you and I would be honest tonight, and give God the credit, you and I could go home tonight and discuss among ourselves what things the Lord has done for us. We all are the recipients of the common grace of God. He has given you life and health and vitality. He has enriched you with many providential blessings. You have employment. You can meet the needs of your wife and family. God , in His goodness, has allowed you to have a roof over your head. And, it has never crossed your mind that that is the doing of the Lord. He is good to you.

But, the Lord didn't tell this man to go home and tell what things the Lord has done for you. Jesus said for the man to go home and tell what GREAT things the Lord has done for you.

There is something greater than common grace. There is something greater than the general goodness of God to all. There is this, the entrance of Jesus into your life and into your lostness. He comes to a life that is barren and empty and godless, and He has come and given you a thirst for Himself, The wonder that He has broken your bond with sin, your desire for sin, and has replaced it with a desire for Himself. That's a great thing! There is a wonder to the grace of God. Tell them what great things He has done for you.

Finally, go home to your friends and TELL them. Conversion doesn't break your relationship with your family and your friends. When a boy in a family of five is converted, it doesn't mean he ceases to be a brother. It means the exact opposite. He has never been a brother in the true sense of that word, to love as a brother. When a husband is converted, it doesn't mean he ceases to be a husband to his wife. He has never been a better husband.

C. H. Spurgeon used to have a vestry hour after the service in which anyone who wanted to could come and see him. People could come and discuss any problem. One night a young man came to see Spurgeon. He claimed to have been converted under Spurgeon's ministry. Spurgeon asked him, "Have you gone home to tell what the Lord has done for you?" The young man said, "Oh, no! I fell out with my father years ago." Spurgeon said, "You go back home and you restore that relationship with your father." Spurgeon wouldn't admit anyone into membership of the church unless relationships were restored by the grace of God with all whom they were connected.

This is what grace does. It restores broken relationships. I know there are people , when they are converted to Christ, who have relationships that are broken. I know there are people who go home and say, "I've been converted", and the people at home don't want them. If you have been going to places you should not go, and you are converted, then there might be broken relationships there. But, the converted still has something to tell them.

Perhaps, for you tonight, this might be the most difficult task of all. I can understand people who find it far easier to come to Christ where no one knows them, rather than on a street where everyone knows them.

It is far easier to witness to those who haven't a clue who you are, rather than witness to those who know you better than anyone else.

This will be the most difficult place for you to begin. Go home and tell them.

What kind of home do you have to go home to tonight? Is it a home that would be glad to hear this testimony? It may be. On the other hand, it might not be. It may be a home where no one has prayed for you, no one has read the Bible to you, no one there would ever think of bringing you to church. No one there would ever think of telling you about the Christian faith. It will be difficult. But, that is where you begin. Go home and tell them.

If you are telling your story to people who are enemies of Christ, and people who tend to laugh at you, let me tell you how to deal with them. Tell them individually. Take them away from the group. It's easy to be brave where there are two or three, but when you are isolated , and on your own, and you're face to face with someone who has something to tell you of the grace of God, it's not so easy for the individual to laugh at you. He's a coward at heart. Witness to the individual.

Then, start enlarging the circle.

Third, get strength to do it. One of these days, who

knows, you might stand in a place like this, and tell people what great things the Lord has done for you.

It is far easier to stand up and tell a congregation like this, than to tell the one or the two or the three. But, the thing is, you go and tell them.

You will never have a greater privilege in this world than to respond to this challenge and this command of Jesus.

Tell people what He has done for you. Tell it humbly. You didn't deserve anything from His hand.

Tell it gently! Tell it graciously! Tell it willingly! Tell it lovingly! Tell it in such a way that you want them to tell the same thing themselves.

Go home and tell them what great things the Lord has done for you. Remember this, one day you are going home. One day you are going to your home above, to heaven where Jesus Himself is. And, you are going to spend eternity telling Him, and those who are with you, what great things the Lord did for you.

That is the song of the redeemed in heaven tonight. To Him who loved us, and washed us from our sins in His own blood, unto Him be glory forever and ever.

You know I end my sermons with a question. My question tonight is very simple. My friend, here tonight, do you have a story to tell? Is there anything at all you could tell anybody about the great things the Lord Jesus Christ has done for you?

If you weren't allowed to speak of anything else tonight but that, would your life be characterized by silence? Do you have anything to tell about the power of His grace? (5)

That Sunday night, in the Free Church of Stornoway, when Murdo Alex Macleod finished preaching this sermon, the congregation sang Psalm 66:16-20

God, in His sovereign wisdom, chose to dip down and cast His grace on the Free Church in Stornoway from 1984-86. Our God is a gracious God.

Rev. Murdo Alex Macleod

Chapter twelve

"THE ISLE OF LEWIS TODAY"
(EILEAN LEODHAS AN-DIUGH)

When one takes a look at what God has done on the Isle of Lewis during the last 180 years, there always arises the eternal question, "Does God do this in other places in the world?" Every place I go to preach in America, people ask the same question, "Is God sending revival over this world? Is revival occurring today?" The answer is, YES! God does bend low over other points. He visits in power and glory on different people. I want to share with you five different places of revival with which I have come in contact in the past few years. The places are different, the people are different, but the same God showers His glory down on His people. Revival is a wonderful mystery known only to God. The Wind of God may come sweeping into a church, a community, or a country. The outpouring of the Spirit of God may last a day, a week, or years. As you read the following stories of revival, pray that God might come in your church, your community in great power.

CARSON-NEWMAN COLLEGE

Alga Hitchcock is the Director of Intercessory Prayer at the First Baptist Church, Altus, Oklahoma. After she had read my first book, "Catch the Wind", she told me the following story.

In 1950, Alga was a student at Carson-Newman College in Jefferson City, Tennessee. At that time, her maiden name was Alga Motychak. She was deeply involved in Christian activities on the campus. They began to hear reports of a great revival on the Isle of Lewis in the Hebrides Islands. This revival began on the Isle of Lewis in December, 1949. This was the first time she had ever heard of Duncan Campbell, the Scottish Highlander preacher of the Lewis Revival.

A group of students on campus began to pray for revival.

They set up a 24-hour prayer chain. Alga chose the fifteen minutes beginning at 2:15 A.M. She chose this time because no one else had taken it, and she wanted to be very spiritual. At the first prayer time, she prayed for everyone and everything she could think of , and still had twelve minutes of her fifteen minutes left. Alga said, “I found out that I didn’t know how to pray.”

But, she began to learn to pray. Suddenly, wonderfully, the Holy Spirit of God moved onto the campus of Carson-Newman College. It was one of those times that can only be explained by the power and grace of God.

When the dust had settled, there had been 444 decisions for Christ, most of them students. However, some of the professors also found eternal life through Jesus Christ. A music professor, whom everyone thought was surely a Christian, came to know Jesus Christ as Savior.

Another professor, who did not know the Lord, came to faith in Jesus Christ in a most unusual way. There was a place where students would leave their books in open cubicles. Students would leave everything there; books, purses, wallets, etc. One day this professor noticed that someone had left an expensive pen in one of the cubicles, lying on top of some books. The professor would walk by, time and time again, noticing the pen was still there. He begin to think, “That pen hasn’t been stolen. If Christianity can do that for a person, there must be something to it.” That professor came to know Christ because of that expensive pen.

It is interesting and wonderful to hear the rest of Alga’s story. From that first fifteen-minute prayer time in 1950, her prayer life grew and grew in intensity. Fifty-two years later, her prayer life reached its pinnacle. On February 20, 2002, a custodian at the church came to Alga’s house, beat her severely, locked her in the trunk of her car, drove out into the country and left her for dead in the trunk. She spent the next 21 hours praying in the trunk of the car. The next day, February 21st, she was discovered and rescued.

God sprinkles His power across the world. Who would ever have dreamed that the stirrings of God on the Isle of Lewis in 1949-53 would find their way to the campus of Carson-Newman College in Tennessee? But, that is how God works. He surprises us with Himself. (1)

FIRST BAPTIST CHURCH, CARTER, OKLAHOMA

Tucked away in the wheat and cotton fields of western Oklahoma is the small town of Carter, with a population of 500-600 people. In 1952, the Spirit of God came down in a remarkable way on that little town. The Pastor of the First Baptist Church, Carter, at that time was Whitley Garrett. He had scheduled a two-week revival meeting. He had invited the Pastor of the First Baptist Church, Erick, Oklahoma to be the preacher for the week. The preacher's name was Dan Beltz.

A small group of men in the Carter church had been meeting in a small room at the church for some time to pray. The prayer meetings would last far into the night as they prayed for God to visit with them.

When the meeting began, suddenly, the fire of God fell on the church, and on the community. The Pastor, Whitley Garrett said he had never seen anything like it in all of his life. Numbers of people were converted to Christ. The preacher, Dan Beltz, was in the habit of taking a long walk every morning. In the two weeks of the meeting, there was not one morning that Beltz was not able to lead someone to Christ during his walk. It was as if God would just put them into his path, without any effort on his part. (2)

One of the converts to Christ during this meeting was a man in the community named George Ridley. He ran a service station in town, had no use for God at all. The men of the church had witnessed to George many times, but to no avail. In the small room at the church, the men would lift George's name to the Heavenly Father. They agonized over him, calling on God to save George Ridley.

One night, during the two-week meeting, George took his hunting dogs south of Carter to the river. He was going Coon hunting. He got his dogs out of his truck, started walking down the river. Sometime, after midnight, the hills and the ground George was walking on began to shake violently. George fell to his knees, and called on God. He didn't know what to do, but he knew where to go to find help. He left his dogs, and ran to his truck. He drove straight to the First Baptist Church. It was 1:30 in the morning. He walked into the church, back to that small room. There in the room was that small group of men on their knees praying. They introduced George to the Lord Jesus Christ, and he was saved.

Shortly after his conversion to Christ, George Ridley was called to preach. He spent the rest of his life as a Baptist Pastor. (3)

This two-week meeting had an impact on the Carter church for years to come. Men and women who were converted during that time are still faithful to the Lord.

DUMAS, TEXAS

It was a small, insignificant non-denominational church in Dumas, Texas. On Sunday morning, the church would have about thirty people in attendance. In the Fall of 2001, the Pastor of this little church decided to have a one-week revival meeting. He invited an evangelist from the state of Washington to preach. The meeting started. Nothing unusual was happening. About the middle of that week, suddenly, the fire of God fell on that little church. Before the week was finished, the building was crowded to capacity. They decided to continue for a second week. During the second week, people were standing outside, listening through open windows. A third week was added. People began to come from all over the Texas Panhandle, the Oklahoma Panhandle, and southern Kansas to attend the meeting. The church installed speakers in every Sunday School room. The crowds grew and grew. People were being saved in every service. The meeting continued for ten weeks. I received my last report on this spiritual awakening ten months after the meeting began. At that point, 550 people had been converted to Christ. (4)

How do we explain this? We don't! It is just a special time when God decides to visit a place in all of His glory.

TYLER, TEXAS

In 1988, Sherman Mayfield was Pastor of the Pleasant Hill Baptist Church in Tyler, Texas. At the time, the church would have an attendance of about 700 on Sunday morning. It was a typical, average Sunday morning. There had been no special emphasis, no type of campaign. Sherman started to church at 7:30 A.M. On the way to church, he suddenly started weeping. This was very unusual for Sherman. He wept all the way to church. When he arrived, he got a broom and began sweeping off the front porch of the church, weeping all the time.

The Sunday School hour was quite normal, except Sherman kept weeping, and did not know why. When he walked into the auditorium for the morning worship service, he immediately noticed people he had never seen before. There were also several lost people to whom the church had been witnessing for a long time.

Sherman stood to preach from Ezekiel 9:1-8. The emphasis of his sermon was on verse 8, "And I was left." He kept weeping through his sermon, as he kept telling the people that when the Lord comes, many will be left. He continued asking the question, "Will you be one of them?"

When Sherman gave the invitation, he said it looked as if the entire congregation flooded to the front of the church. It seemed as if the Holy Spirit was working in the hearts of everyone present, the saved and the lost.

The invitation lasted for an hour. When the service closed, there had been sixty-five people converted to Christ, plus numbers of people who rededicated their lives to the Lord, and many, many who came to confess and repent privately.

That night, there were twenty-five more people who were converted to Christ. At the close of the Sunday night service, Sherman Mayfield, the Pastor, told the congregation that he did not know what was happening, but he would continue to preach as long as the Holy Spirit was moving. The services continued through Wednesday night. A total of one hundred and sixteen people were converted to Christ during those four days.

Sherman Mayfield said, "There was such a freshness of the Holy Spirit during those days. That freshness should be normal, but it happened, and then was over in a week's time." (5)

SOUTHWEST BAPTIST ASSEMBLY

When God comes down in all of His glory, it can last for

years, months, a week, or a day. When real revival comes from God, it may only last for a few hours. God, in His sovereignty, does as He pleases.

Tucked away in the southwestern part of the state of Oklahoma are the Wichita Mountains. At the foot of one of these mountains is the Southwest Baptist Assembly, a church campground which is owned by several Baptist churches and Baptist associations of Southwest Oklahoma.

In July, 2004, five churches from a local Baptist Association took their children to Southwest Baptist Assembly for a church camp. The camp was four days in length. There were a total of 140 campers, including adult sponsors and children. The children ranged in age from ten to thirteen.

The camp pastor was Randy Allen, Pastor of the First Baptist Church, Lindsay, Oklahoma. When he was first invited to be the camp pastor, he declined because he did not feel his gift was in preaching to children. When he was approached a second time, he consented to preach at the camp.

The first two nights of the camp were a bit wooden and empty. Randy did not feel a sense of the power of God. The third and last night proved to be quite different.

That third and last night of the camp, Randy preached from the 21st chapter of the Gospel of John, where Jesus asked, "Peter, do you love me?" When the invitation was extended, Randy felt the same emptiness, no power, no sense of the wonderful presence of God. Then, SUDDENLY, HE came. The precious Lord invaded the meeting.

Randy Allen said the only way he could explain what happened was by referring to a movie from some years back. In 1991, the movie, "Backdraft", came out. It was the story of firefighters who were battling huge fires. The title of the movie, "Backdraft", refers to a condition where the fire builds and builds in heat and intensity. The fire is smoldering, and mostly hidden. Then, the fire finally explodes into a deadly rage when the slightest hint of oxygen is introduced.

That is how Randy Allen described what happened next. Suddenly, everyone in the congregation began to weep, adults as well as children. The invitation lasted for one hour. When the worship service was finally dismissed, thirty-six people had been converted to Christ.

However, it was not over! The service was dismissed, but the people would not leave. They stayed for some time, weeping and crying out to God. Two hours after the people had left, the camp music director went to one of the cabins. When he walked into the cabin, the adult sponsors and children were sitting around weeping before God. That is revival! (6)

When you look back at 180 years of revival on the Isle of Lewis, you are struck by several things. You notice that all revival movements are different. No two revivals are alike. God comes down in all of His glory in different fashion. The way God drew men and women to Himself in 1827 in the village of Uig was different to the way He did it in Barvas in 1949. Revivals are like snowflakes; no two are exactly alike.

Yet, with all their differences, there are commonalities in revival. God may adorn Himself in different manners to different people in different times, but there are certain things that remain timeless in revival.

As I have studied the different revival movements on Lewis, I have been captured by the essential ingredients in each of the revival movements. In every revival on Lewis there was always prayer. As prayer increased, there always came a brokenness, a cry, "O God, are my hands clean? Is my heart pure?" When brokenness came, it was always followed by deep, abiding repentance and confession of sin. Prayer, brokenness, repentance, and confession was always followed by wonderful, life-changing conversion of the lost.

The prayers of the people of Lewis are vastly different from the prayers of the people of America. On the Isle of Lewis, prayers are long and involved. They are not only petitions and requests, but they are masterpieces of praise and glorifying Almighty God. I think it would be worthwhile to look at one of the prayers of a Lewisman. The following prayer was prayed in church by the Rev. Murdo Alex Macleod. You need to understand, there is no difference in the prayer of a minister and a layman. Both pray with insight, great biblical knowledge, and wonderful passion. Listen as this minister prays:

"O, Lord, our God, we thank Thee that we can make mention of Thy goodness. Thou hast given us the privilege of extolling Thy name and declaring Thy works. Give us thankful hearts tonight, that the rest which went before us, that that rest made mention of Thy greatness to us. And, we bless Thee for the promise that is attached to the proclamation of Thy Word and to all who witness to the grace and saving power of God.

We pray that Thy Word will not return to you void, and can prosper in that to which you have sent it, and can accomplish the purpose you have for it. And, we bless Thy name, O Lord, that that Word is effective in the hand of the Spirit as it has been in past ages. We bless Thee that the works which were done by Thee in days of old, which our fathers have told us of, we bless Thee that they were able to accomplish that work in our day. For, Thou art the same God. Thy hand is great in might. There is no change with Thee. There is no diminishing of Thy power. And, we bless Thee, O Lord, that that is an encouragement as we lift our hearts to Thee here this night, in this act of worship.

We call upon the name of the Living God, the God of Abraham, the God of Isaac, and the God of Jacob, the God of the living , the God who calls out of darkness and sustains them by His grace, the God who calls by His power, men and women, boys and girls, out of the darkness of sin, and from the enslaving power of evil. And, though we know that the forces of darkness and of evil wage a consistent and constant war against Thee, we bless your name that Thou art enthroned on high. And, though there are the powers of darkness, and the power of the prince of this world, a power which is far greater than any of us, or all of us together, yet, that power is limited by Thee. For, Thou art the God of all power, the God of all grace. And, to Thee, in Thy mercy this night, come forth in saving power, through the medium that Thou hast appointed, the proclamation of the gospel of Thy love. For God was in Christ reconciling the world unto Himself. And Thou hast entrusted to man the proclamation of that gospel. We pray that as it is proclaimed throughout the length and breadth of our land this evening, and as it is proclaimed throughout the world, that Christ may see the travail of a soul and be satisfied.

We bless Thy Holy Name, that all He died to accomplish will be fulfilled. We thank Thee that the day is going to dawn when He will have the preeminence, when His kingdom will extend from sea to sea. O Lord, will Thou grant a hearing ear to the petitions of those who love Thy name, when they pray tonight, that souls will be saved under the preaching of the gospel. And, that Thy people will be edified and encouraged in the exercise of their faith.

We bless Thee, O Lord, for what Thou art able to accomplish. We bless Thee, that Thy arm is not shortened, that it cannot save, Thine ear is not heavy, that it cannot hear. And, wilt Thou anoint all Thy servants tonight with the unction of the Holy Spirit, so that the gospel will go forth in power, and in demonstration of the Spirit. We thank Thee, O Lord, for its relevance and its permanence, the message that is always new, and the offer that is extended with so much meaning, blessing and favor attached to it, and accompanied by it. We bless Thee for the reality of the power of God in the lives of individuals and families and communities. And, we pray that Thou would strengthen that reality in our own midst, that Thou would make the cause of Christ stronger than it ever was.

We bemoan the spiritual declension that has overtaken us, and we grieve at the lack of spiritual life and vitality. We beseech Thee, O Lord, to stir us up, so that we would arrest that decline in dependency upon Thy grace. Lord, strengthen every evidence of vital religion in our midst, and grant that we would see a resurgence and a reemergence of its place in the life of our nation. Have mercy upon us. Have mercy upon those who claim to lead us in parliament and local affairs. And, we pray that Thou would strengthen the heart and hands of those who honor Thy name and Thy law in our midst.

And would Thou grant, O Lord, that we would see Thy power manifested, the forces of evil thwarted. We know, Lord, that their voice is becoming more and more powerful in our midst. And, we know the voice of those who clamor for changes which are not in accordance with Thy law, is a voice which is a minority in our land, and yet, the opportunity is given to them, and taken by them to present the claims as though they were in the majority. And, as though all they seek to do is so normal and in harmony with a lifestyle which is normal, we know from Thy Word that it is an abomination in Thy presence, an abomination to the many in this land who respect

Thy Word, and who respect the life that Thy Word presents and commends to each one of us.

Lord, our God, deliver us from evil, we pray Thee. Bless us here this night, our homes, our families. Bless our young away from home. Have mercy upon them. We pray that Thou wilt undertake in mercy those who are laid sick at home in illness, or in the hospital. Sanctify Thy sovereign dealings with them, and upon those who mourn over the loss of loved ones. Give us, now, an ear for Thy gospel, O Lord. Draw near to us, and shed light to us upon the meaning of Thy Word, and apply it with conviction, with the convicting power of the Holy Spirit, to our hearts, so that Thy name might be glorified and our souls benefited. For Jesus' sake, Amen! (7)

As I have studied the different revival movements on Lewis, I have looked for a central theme in those revivals. I have wondered if there was a central truth proclaimed that made them possible. It is true that the preachers in these revivals preached with great power on the "terror of the Lord." In the Lewis Revival of 1949-53, the predominant message of Duncan Campbell in the church meetings was on the wrath of God and the judgment of God. However, when the people who were interested in coming to Christ would retire to the "kitchen meetings" in one of the homes, Campbell would speak to them at every "kitchen meeting" on, "My sheep hear My voice, and I know them, and they follow me. And I give them eternal life, and they shall never perish; neither shall anyone snatch them out of My hand" (John 10:27-28). If you had to pick out a central theme of the preaching of the Lewis Revivals, you would probably pick the abiding love of God for those who are lost from Him.

It has been an intriguing thing for me, as I have searched

through the history of revival on Lewis, to discover the extreme importance of the Communion Season. In a certain sense, the Communion Season has been the springboard of revival on the island. The Communion Season would always be held twice a year. Visiting ministers would be invited to come and preach. People would stream toward that particular church from all over the island. The saved and the lost would come. Why did the Communion Season contribute to revival? It may have been a time when the minds of the people would be more open to the thoughts of God. The hearts of believers would be in a most tender state, and all the people, lost and saved, would hear the essential, central message of the Gospel of Jesus Christ.

There have been many, down through the years, who have either denounced the revivals on the Isle of Lewis, or else have denied the revivals. There has been the accusation that the revivals have occurred among the ignorant and the unlearned. Those who take this avenue have said that the unusual manifestations of the revivals such as prostrations, and other physical manifestations could only come from the wells of ignorance. No educated, well-learned person would ever get caught up in such a thing.

It is a matter of true history that most of the ministers on the Isle of Lewis were well educated. The people of Lewis after the Revival of 1824-28 became well-learned people. To accuse them of ignorance is to rewrite history.

To look at the unusual events of the revivals on Lewis is to see prostrations, visions, physical manifestations. These things seem strange and uncommon to people living in the 21st Century. In the Lewis Revival of 1949-53, a young man was converted to Christ one night at a dance in Carloway. His name was Allan Macarthur. Out of his experience with Christ, his father, mother, and five siblings came to faith in Jesus Christ. Allan Macarthur and his brother, Jack, became Church of Scotland ministers. Today, Allan Macarthur is retired and living in Lochcarron, Scotland. Allan Macarthur said, "I remember hearing as a young boy of the move of God's Spirit in the small Free Church at Garyvard (a few miles from where I was born). Tongues of fire were seen by some in the church, and people were being carried out and laid on the grass outside. It has always remained with me. Of course, some attributed it to the work of the devil, but, when later on in life I began to study what happened at Pentecost, I have wondered if this was not something similar."(8) There is one thing for certain: In the midst of the prostrations, the visions, the physical manifestations, the people never lost sight of the central message of revival. The people kept their eyes focused on the centrality of Jesus Christ.

People question these events. Did they really happen? If they did happen, were such things of God? We should remember the people to whom these things happened. The people of the Isle of Lewis have traditionally been people of a most reserved nature. They are a private, quiet, gentle, reticent people. To believe that the people of Lewis would fall down in a public worship service on their own is to not know these dear people. To believe that they would weep, sob loudly, cry out to God in public is to have no understanding of the nature of the Lewisman or Lewiswomen.

The people of Lewis are a reserved, dignified people. Their idea of public worship is quiet, reserved, without emotion whatsoever. In fact, the usual worship service in a church on Lewis would be called staid and wooden. But, when God came, the people came alive. Hearts were broken! Tears were shed! A long pent-up cry was heard! Singing the praises of God became totally common in churches, on roads, in buses. Everywhere people were talking about God! No wonder God manifested Himself in unusual ways.

The unusual events in the revivals on the Isle of Lewis happened to people who were truly seeking an Eternal, Living God. They happened to a people who were deadly earnest in what they were doing.

Something else that I have found interesting as I have looked at these different revival movements on the Isle of Lewis is the connection between them. As revival came again and again to Lewis, one can catch a glimpse of the thread that connects one to the other. Those who were the preachers in one revival movement would produce children, or grandchildren who would be the preachers in a later revival. The converts and leaders of one revival movement would produce sons and daughters who would be soldiers of the Cross in the next revival movement. You can still see that thread of connection today on Lewis. Those who were converted to Christ during the Lewis Revival of 1949-53 have a deep, passionate desire to see it again.

One thing that may have played a large part in the many revivals that have come to Lewis is the family devotion. Over three hundred years ago there became stamped on the minds of the Scottish people the importance, or necessity of having a family devotion. For generations, it became the standard practice, the tradition for each family, lost and saved, to have family devotion morning and night. In this family devotion, a portion of the Bible would be read, and a prayer offered. If the father of the home was absent, the mother would take the Bible, read a passage, then offer a prayer before the children would go to bed.

The Bible was also a common Book in the schools of

Lewis. The Bible was read, studied and memorized by the children in school.

Mary Morrison, a young lady who was converted to Christ in the Lewis Revival of 1949-53, later became a Pilgrim with the Faith Mission. Mary was one of the young ladies instrumental in the revival that came to the Island of North Uist in 1957-58. Mary Morrison married Colin Peckham, who served for many years as the Principal of the Faith Mission College.

Mary Morrison grew up on the north end of the Isle of Lewis near the village of Ness. Mary said, "As a child I was accustomed to family worship each morning, not only in our home, but sometimes in the home of friends, or my grandparents. It was the normal thing in the homes of our villages, as far as I knew, to have morning daily worship. That doesn't mean that all the people in the village were Christians, but they had promised in the church to bring up their children in the nurture and fear and admonition of the Lord, and they felt that this was part and parcel of fulfilling that promise. So many unconverted parents in that village, including my own, thought it was right to read the Word of God to their family, and to pray. I can't say that I listened very carefully to the reading of the Word. I really wasn't at all attentive. It was just part of life. In school we would start out each day with the Lord's Prayer, and then went on to Bible stories and the Presbyterian Shorter Catechism. On most days, we would come home from school with a verse from the Psalms to learn. So you can see that our people were well-versed in the Scriptures. We knew the Ten Commandments by heart. We also knew Isaiah 53 and 55, the Beatitudes, I Corinthians 13, and many others. Even though an unconverted people, we were not strangers to the Word of God.

When the Spirit of God fell on our island, there was fuel there to burn." (9)

Family devotions became an igniter to the people of Lewis. When the Wind of God began to blow, the Word of God, hidden in the hearts of the people from family devotions, exploded and brought revival.

Another thing that has come out of the revivals on the Isle of Lewis is a strict Sabbatarianism. Throughout the last 200 years, there has evolved a sense of legalism in the churches of Lewis that some believe has plagued the churches.

Some of the unwritten rules of legalism that were observed were:

1. One could carry a bucket of water from the door to the fireplace on the Sabbath, but one could not carry water from the well into the house.
2. No cooking was to be done on Sunday. All of the food eaten on Sunday had to be cooked on Saturday.
3. The men shaved on Saturday night. It was considered breaking the laws of the Sabbath to shave on Sunday.
4. Men had to wear black suit, black shoes, and white shirts on the Sabbath. One minister who opposed Duncan Campbell and the Lewis Revival of 1949-53 once met Duncan Campbell. He said, "I ran into the plague today. Just as I thought! He was wearing brown shoes." (10)
5. Duncan Matheson, minister at Knock and Gairloch, had a friend whom he regarded as a son. The friend had to catch a ferry to go to the Island of Skye. The ferry left Stornoway at a very early hour on Monday morning. The friend boarded the ferry late on Sabbath night. Mr. Matheson heard about it and suspended his friend from church membership for a year (11)
6. You could brush your coat if it had specks of dust, but you

could not touch your boot if it had a splash of mud.

Donald Ross was one of the "Men of Lewis." It is said of him, "He was a man of big principles and disliked details of application that were arbitrary and meaningless. He bravely drew fresh water from the well on the Sabbath, and did other things with no local sanction, but no man was more loyal than he to the law of Christ." (12)

Through the years, the Isle of Lewis has been quite strict about its observance of the Sabbath. Businesses closed! No work was done! No business was transacted! Ferries shut down! Planes did not fly!

Much of this Sabbatarianism seems to be changing on Lewis today. When I was on the Isle of Lewis, I attended church at Barvas. I was cautioned by a minister on the mainland of Scotland to wear a black suit, black shoes, and a white dress shirt to church. On the night I attended, I was the only man there with a white dress shirt on. All the other men had on colored dress shirts.

When I was on Lewis in October, 2001, businesses were closed on Sabbath, planes did not fly into or out of Stornoway. The ferries did not run on the Sabbath. But, things are changing. In the past few weeks I have noticed an article in the Stornoway Gazette newspaper that planes are beginning to fly to one of the islands of Sunday. There has come a slackening of the rules. One lady of Lewis told me, "Yes, it is not as strict as it once was, but there was a certain peace and calmness on the Sabbath. Everything was quiet. Cars were not running up and down the road. There was a serenity about the Sabbath."

What is happening on the Isle of Lewis today? Is revival happening? What is the condition of the churches?

I realize that I may not have the knowledge or the

authority to speak on this matter. I am not of Lewis. I am an AOkie" from Oklahoma in America. I only can write about the things I have read, the people to whom I have spoken, and the things I have observed.

There is still spiritual life in the churches on the Isle of Lewis. However, it is a different story concerning the churches on the mainland of Scotland. Churches are declining, some closing their doors, others are merging, trying to garner enough people to have church. When I was preaching in Greenock, Scotland in May, 2002, I read an article in the local newspaper. The article spoke of five Churches of Scotland in Greenock that were meeting together the following Sunday, making final plans for a merger into one church. I asked the Minister of the church where I was preaching what this meant. He told me this was happening all over Scotland. Churches with huge buildings, splendid histories, who were now merging, trying to find enough people to keep the church doors open.

It is best to let a man of Scotland tell the story. Dr. Colin Peckham served for many years as the Principal of the Faith Mission College in Edinburgh, Scotland. Dr. Peckham said this concerning the state of the church in Scotland:

"The tide is out! The rocks protrude from the muddy waters, ugly and bare. Stretches of muddy sand mar the former beauty. Footprints show the progress of hopeful mussel, cockle and seafood collectors. The tide is out!

Nothing attractive about the tide being out is there! No living waters, swelling, swirling, crashing, breaking against those cold, grey stones, overcoming and submerging them in their heady conquest. No fish darting through the rising waves. No shouts and laughter from the happy swimmers. No. The tide is out!

In Great Britain today, the tide is out! It is normal to have but a few people at our meetings. Churches are being closed as congregations merge. The national church loses thousands every year and has done so for many years. Growth is abnormal. We have settled for death! A few weeks ago I preached in a church whose attendance had dropped from 800 to 80 in the past twenty years. That's expected. People don't bother about church these days. The tide is out!

The present young generation knows nothing different. They don't know the moving of the waters; they have experienced so very little of the glory of God descending upon a meeting. Rarely have they known the melting pressure of a mighty God breaking through into the midst where tears flow freely, and where lives are transformed forever. They just don't know about it. The tide is out!

Poor Great Britain, once the tide was in and we were a blessing to the whole world; now the tide is out and we are spiritually bankrupt. Worst of all, we don't know it! We have forsaken the Word of the Lord.....

All we can do is to bend and gather our meager cockles and mussels. They will keep some of us alive, fewer and fewer of us. It's a back-breaking job to keep on gathering cockles and mussels; it's a soul-destroying task to keep on preaching to people who have rejected the message you bring and have already passed into the godless vacuum of a materialistic post-Christian era. They don't want what you bring, and the coldness and indifference of the world has penetrated the very fellowships which once were expanding with vibrant life. The tide is out! Ichabod!

Is this the end of the road? Will darkness ultimately settle upon England's green and pleasant land, upon Scotland's majestic mountains? Will the grandeur of their history, the glory of their past merely become a fading memory until it passes quite out of mind and out of sight? Will England's darkness and Scotland's hardness become complete?

No! The tide must turn. For those who are watching on the walls of Zion, the tide is turning. Not significantly at all-no. But it would seem that there are gleams of light here and there, very small gleams, but there is light, hopeful, inspiring light. In the darkness, God's promises shine brightest. (13)

There are many believers in Scotland today who feel the state of the church in Scotland has declined to such a degree that apostasy is in the near future. There are groups in Scotland who are praying fervently for revival.

When I was in Scotland in 2001, I attended church on Sunday morning in the rural church where Duncan Campbell grew up, just north of Oban, Scotland. The massive, magnificent building would set from 500-600 people. Its past was one of glory and honor to God. This building had seen revival. It had known the power of God within its walls. That Sunday morning, there were 33 people in attendance, and I was shocked at the worship service. I have never attended a more wooden, dead, dull church service in my life. There was no word about Jesus Christ, no mention of the Cross of Christ, no message of salvation. There were only a few songs, some words from the preacher about giving more money, then.......NOTHING. I went away from that service depressed in spirit, wondering if the revival days of the past would ever return to a place like this.

I sense something different on the Isle of Lewis. Although the church on Lewis is suffering a low state right now, I do sense a desire to know again the spirit of revival.

THE CHURCH IN BARVAS

Barvas! That word rings with the sounds of revival. It was in this building God came down in all of His glory one night in December, 1949. Duncan Campbell was preaching. Barvas! That little village had known great revival in 1939 when unusual men and women of prayer had caught the attention of God, and had called down the power of God on that region.

Today in Barvas church attendance is low, and the Spirit of God is not moving as He has in the past, but there are groanings of the Spirit going on in Barvas. When I visited with some of the people of Barvas in 2001, each one I talked to said the same thing, "We want to see it again." There is a remnant of people still left in Barvas who know and understand revival. They have seen it, and have felt it. And that connection is there, that connection! The children and grandchildren of the men and women who have known revival in the past are still there. They have the stamp of revival on their souls.

The present minister of the Barvas Church is Tommy Macneil. Macneil was installed as minister in February, 2002. He is a man who has a heart for revival. In an E-mail to me, Tommy said, "The people of Barvas are once again having prayer meetings in their homes until 1:00 and 2:00 in the mornings. They are earnestly seeking revival. The Wind of God is beginning to blow once again in Barvas."

Revival has not come again to Barvas, but I do believe it is coming. God has not left the land He has chosen to love. He will once again come in power on tiny Barvas.

THE CHURCH IN UIG

Uig, the isolated, hidden corner of the Isle of Lewis. That place where the Spirit of God has come so strongly in the past. Uig, where Rev. Alexander Macleod came as minister in 1824, and the glory of God came down. To remember that in 1827, 9,000 to 11,000 people gathered on that hillside for Communion Season in Uig, and the glory of God was so strong, that as they sang a Psalm, only two ministers and the precentor were singing. The people could do nothing but sob uncontrollably .

Today in Uig, the Rev. William Macleod is the minister. In February, 2004, the church and community celebrated Rev. Macleod's 40th anniversary as minister of the church in Uig. Rev. Macleod and his wife are well acquainted with revival. They know it, and have seen it. Both of them were converted to Christ during the Barvas revival of 1949-53 under the preaching of Duncan Campbell.

But, the signs of revival are not in Uig now. There were, in the past, three good churches in Uig. Today, there is only one. Rev. Macleod recently said, "It is very much a strong Gaelic congregation, but we have an English service on Sunday mornings and a Gaelic service in the evenings. There are normally between 30 and 60 at the services. We also have an outreach service in the evening for the non-churchgoers and this attracts between 15 and 20.(14)

Will the Wind of God blow again on Uig? I believe it will, but only God knows how and when.

THE CHURCH IN BACK

North of the town of Stornoway, along the east coast of the Isle of Lewis, sits the village of Back. The minister of the

Free Church in Back is the Rev. Iain D. Campbell. It has been my privilege in the last several months to correspond with Rev. Campbell on many occasions. I have also had the opportunity to read several of his writings. I have no reason to say what I am about to say other than it is a feeling deep in my spirit. I believe there is the possibility that revival could come to the Back Church in the near future. I am not sure that I can even relate my reasons for believing this, other than to say that Rev. Campbell has a heart to see God move in all of His power. He preaches the Gospel of Jesus Christ, and, as he wrote, "The church may well be viewed as a disempowered fundamentalism. But it was precisely at times of spiritual barrenness and dearth that the work of the Kingdom of God was fanned into a new flame. We may become discouraged and slip into despair, but the ancient word of the prophet still has something to say to the church: not by might, nor by power, but by my Spirit, says the Lord of hosts.' If we learn that much from the revivals of the past, we will have learned the most important lesson that our history can teach us." (15)

The Isle of Lewis is living with a changing world today. The old ways of life are fading, and new things are invading their society. Some of the new things are good, many are bad. They are losing the "peace of the Sabbath." In this land where crime was almost nonexistent, it is now making its way into the lives of the people of Lewis. In a recent article in the Stornoway Gazette, a Police detective with the Western Isles Police Department talked about the coming of drugs to the Isle of Lewis. In a land where police had little work, where houses and possessions were totally safe at all times, where divorce was unheard of, into this land, the world has come with all of its evils. That is such a shame.

To find an explanation as to why the Isle of Lewis is the

land God chose to love, that is impossible for the human mind. The explanation is wrapped up in the mind of Almighty God, and, perhaps, will be revealed to us when we enter heaven. We don't understand it now. Why would Almighty God pick this place to be the seat of His Shekinah glory? Why would Jehovah select this corner of the world for His fire to fall, again and again. Rev. David Searle said, "I believe that in the Divine Operations Room, where the map is on the wall, marked with forward battalions in that divine conflict with the powers of evil, Bravas is a golden star, one of the choice companies engaging in battle for the Kingdom." (16)

BUT, God is there! And, the Isle of Lewis is still," The Land God Chose to Love." The natural eye of man may see nothing, but, there are people on Lewis who are crying out to God. One of these days I fully expect to see the GLORY OF SCOTLAND to once again rise and claim its place as REVIVAL comes to the Isle of Lewis.

Rev. William Macleod

Rev. Ian Campbell

END NOTES

CHAPTER ONE: "The Land" (An Tir)

1. Macleish, Kenneth. *Scotland's Outer Hebrides*, National Geographic, November, 1974, Page 683
2. Maclean, Fitzroy. *A Concise History of Scotland*, Thames and Hudson Inc., 2000, Page 209
3. Allen, Brad. *Catch the Wind*, Word Association Publishers, 2002, Page 4
4. Campbell, Duncan. *Principles that Govern Spiritual Awakening*, Audio Tape in author's library
5. MacDonald, Donald. *Lewis, a History of the Island*. Edinburgh, Scotland, Gordon Wright Publishing, 1990, Page 69
6. West, Morris. *The Summer of the Red Wolf*, Page 51
7. Ibid. Page 53
8. Taylor, Steve. *The Skye Revivals*, New Wine Press, 2003, Page 37
9. Ibid. Page 38
10. Highland Clearances, Memorial Fund Series
11. Taylor, Steve. *The Skye Revivals*, New Wine Press, 2003, Page 127-28
12. Allen, Brad. *Catch the Wind*, Word Association Publishers, 2002, Page 16
13. Ferguson, John. *When God Came Down*, Lewis Recordings, 2000, Page 26

CHAPTER TWO: "The Revival of 1824-1828" ('Dusgadh 1824-1828)

1. Macaulay, Murdo. *Aspects of the Religious History of Lewis*, John G. Eccles Printers Ltd., Inverness, Page 169
2. Macfarland, Norman. *Apostles of the North*, The Gazette

Office, Stornoway, Page 80

3. Taylor, Steve. *The Skye Revivals*, New Wine Press, 2003, Page 38
4. Monthly Record, September, 1918, Page 163
5. Macfarlane, Norman. *Apostles of the North*, The Gazette Office, Stornoway, Page 73
6. Macaulay, Murdo. *Aspects of the Religious History of Lewis*, John G. Eccles Printers Ltd., Inverness, Page 170
7. Ibid. Page 17
8. Beaton, D. *Some Noted Ministers of the Northern Highlands*, Inverness, Northern Counties Newspaper, 1929, Page 205-06
9. Macaulay, Murdo. *Aspects of the Religious History of Lewis*, John G. Eccles Printers Ltd., Inverness, Page 175
10. Ibid. Page 179
11. Ibid. Page 179
12. Taylor, Steve. *The Skye Revivals*, New Wine Press, 2003, Page 26
13. Macleod, Norman. *Lewis Revivals of the 20th Century*, Hebridean Press Service, Stornoway, 1988, Page 17
14. Macaulay, Murdo. *Aspects of the Religious History of Lewis*, John G. Eccles Printers Ltd., Inverness, Page 194
15. Macfarlane, Norman. *The Men of the Lews*, The Gazette Office, Stornoway, 1924, Page 25
16. Ibid. Page 23
17. Macrae, Alexander. *Revival in the Highlands and Islands*, Tentmaker Publications, Hartshill, Stoke-on-Trent, 1998, Page 87
18. Ibid. Page 86
19. Ibid. Page 87
20. Taylor, Steve. *The Skye Revivals*, New Wine Press, 2003, Page 98

21. Ibid. Page 103
22. Beaton, D. *Some Noted Ministers of the Northern Highlands"*, Inverness, Northern Counties Newspaper, 1929, Page 266
23. Campbell, Murdoch.*Gleanings of Highland Harvest*, Christian Focus Publications, 1953, Page 22
24. Ibid. Page 22
25. Beaton, D. *Some Noted Ministers of the Northern Highlands*, Inverness, Northern Counties Newspaper, 1929, Page 267
26. Stornoway Gazette Newspaper, Stornoway, Isle of Lewis, December 25, 1971
27. Stornoway Gazette Newspaper, Stornoway, Isle of Lewis, January 1, 1972
28. Stornoway Gazette Newspaper, Stornoway, Isle of Lewis, January 22, 1972
29. Stornoway Gazette Newspaper, Stornoway, Isle of Lewis, January 29, 1972
30. Macaulay, Murdo. *Aspects of the Religious History of Lewis*, John G. Eccles Printers Ltd., Inverness. Page 132
31. Ibid. Page 133
32. Ibid. Page 138
33. Ibid. Page 167
34. Beaton, D. *Diary and Sermons of the Rev. Alexander Macleod*, Robert Carruthers And Sons, Inverness, 1925, Page 31-39
35. Sandison, Bruce. *A Trip Back in Time*, Scottish Life Magazine, Autumn, 2004, Page 56
36. Taylor, Steve. *The Skye Revivals*, New Wine Press, 2003, Page 50-51

CHAPTER THREE: "The Revival of 1840-1843" ('Dusgadh 1840-1843)

1. Taylor, Steve. *The Skye Revivals*, New Wine Press, 2003, Page 61
2. Ibid. Page 58-60
3. Macaulay, Murdo. *Aspects of the Religious History of Lewis*, John G. Eccles Printers Ltd., Inverness, Page 204
4. Macaulay, Murdo. *The Burning Bush of Carloway*, Essprint Ltd., Stornoway, 1984, Page 15-16
5. Macaulay, Murdo. *Aspects of the Religious History of Lewis*, John G. Eccles Printers Ltd., Inverness, Page 84
6. Ibid. Page 97
7. Macfarlane, Norman. *Apostles of the North*, The Gazette Office, Stornoway, Page 22
8. Macaulay, Murdo. *Aspects of the Religious History of Lewis*, John G. Eccles Printers Ltd., Inverness, Page 97-98
9. Macfarlane, Norman. *Apostles of the North*, The Gazette Office, Stornoway, Page 25
10. Ibid. Page 24-25

CHAPTER FOUR: "The Revival of 1857-1860" ('Dusgadh 1857-1860)

1. Taylor, Steve. *The Skye Revivals*, New Wine Press, 2003, Page 115
2. Ibid. Page 119
3. Roberts, Richard Owen. *Scotland Saw His Glory*, International Awakening Press, 1995, Page 290
4. Taylor, Steve. *The Skye Revivals*, New Wine Press, 2003, Page 119
5. Roberts, Richard Owen. *Scotland Saw His Glory*, International Awakening Press, 1995, Page 293

6. Macfarlane, Norman. *Apostles of the North*, The Gazette Office, Stornoway, Page 69
7. Campbell, Murdoch. *Gleanings of Highland Harvest*, Christian Focus Publications, 1953, Page 45
8. Collins, G.N.M. *Big Macrae*, Knox Press, Edinburgh, 1976, Page 38
9. Macfarlane, Norman. *Apostles of the North*, The Gazette Office, Stornoway, Page 15

CHAPTER FIVE: "The Revival of 1900-1903" ('Dusgadh 1900-1903)

1. Macleod, Norman. *Lewis Revivals of the 20th Century*, Hebridean Press Service, Stornoway, 1988, Page 6
2. Macrae, Alexander. *Revivals in the Highlands and Islands*, Tentmaker Publications, 1998, Page 88
3. Ibid. Page 90
4. Macleod, Norman. *Lewis Revivals of the 20th Century*, Hebridean Press Service, Stornoway, 1988, Page 8
5. Campbell, Murdoch. *Gleanings of Highland Harvest*, Christian Focus Publications, 1953, Page 49
6. Ibid. Page 51
7. Ibid. Page 51

CHAPTER SIX: The Revival of 1923-1926" ('Dusgadh 1923-1926)

1. Macauley, Murdo. *The Burning Bush of Carloway*, Esspring Ltd., Stornoway, 1984 Page 32
2. Campbell, Murdoch. *Memories of a Wayfaring Man*, Inverness, 1974, Page 10-11
3. Campbell, Iain. *Revival in Lewis*, Article in the Stornoway Gazette, Page 4

CHAPTER SEVEN: "The Revival of 1934-1939" ('Dusgadh 1934-1939)

1. Taylor, Steve. A paper mailed to me by Steve Taylor, resident of the Isle of Skye.
2. Macaulay, Murdo. *The Burning Bush of Carloway*, Essprint Ltd., Stornoway, 1984, Page 33
3. Ibid. Page 33
4. Ibid. Page 33
5. Ibid. Page 34
6. Ibid. Page 39
7. Ibid. Page 40
8. Ibid. Page 42
9. Ibid. Page 45
10. Article from Free Church.Org, Page 2
11. Macaulay, Murdo. *The Burning Bush of Carloway*, Essprint Ltd., Stornoway, 1984, Page 50
12. Ibid. Page 51
13. Ibid. Page 52
14. Ibid. Page 53
15. Macaulay, Murdo and Macleod, Murdo Alex. *Discussion on Revival*, Audio tape in author's library.
16. Taylor, Steve. A paper sent to me by Steve Taylor. This comes from the end notes on that Paper.
17. Stornoway Gazette Newspaper, June 2, 1939
18. Black, Hugh. *The Clash of Tongues with Glimpses of Revival*, New Dawn Books, Greenock, Scotland, 1988, Page 127-28
19. Ibid. Page 138-153
20. Campbell, Duncan. Audio Tape in author's library
21. Black, Hugh. *The Clash of Tongues with Glimpses of Revival*, New Dawn Books, Greenock, Scotland, 1988, Page 129-30

CHAPTER EIGHT: "The Revival of 1949-1953" ('Dusgadh 1949-1953)

1. Campbell, Duncan. *Testimony*, audio tape in author's library
2. Campbell, Duncan. Tape #4, audio tape in author's library
3. Ibid.
4. Ibid
5. Ibid.
6. Campbell, Duncan. *When the Fire of God Fell*, audio tape in author's library
7. Campbell, Duncan. *The Lewis Revival*, audio tape in author's library
8. Ibid.
9. Campbell, Duncan. *When the Fire of God Fell*, audio tape in author's library
10. Ibid.
11. Ibid.
12. Campbell, Duncan. *The Lewis Revival*, audio tape in author's library
13. Ibid.
14. Ibid.
15. Stornoway Gazette Newspaper, December, 1949
16. Campbell, Duncan. *The Lewis Revival*, audio tape in author's library
17. Ibid.
18. Ibid.
19. Ibid.
20. Ibid.
21. Campbell, Duncan. *Principles that Govern Spiritual Awakening*, audio tape in Author's library
22. Campbell, Duncan. *Tape #2*. Audio tape in author's library
23. Ibid.

24. Peckham, Colin. *Sounds from Heaven*, Christian Focus Publications, Fearn, Scotland, 2004, Page 82
25. Ibid. Page 214
26. *The Wind of the Spirit,* Ambassador Publications, Ireland. Video tape in author's Library

CHAPTER NINE: "The Revival of 1960-1965" ('Dusgadh 1960-1965)

1. Effrey, Kenneth. *When the Lord Walked the Land*, Paternoster Press, 2002, Page 2
2. Ferguson, John. *When God Came Down*, Lewis Recordings, 2000, Page 14
3 Personal letter to author, from a Baptist Pastor in England, February 29, 2004
4. Macleod, Norman. *Lewis Revivals of the 20th Century*, Hebridean Press Service, Stornoway, 1988, Page 16
5. Campbell, Iain. *Revival in Lewis'*, An article written by Iain Campbell on December 30, 2003

CHAPTER TEN: "The Revival of 1969-1973" ('Dusgadh 1969-1973)

1. Peckham, Colin. *Sounds from Heaven*, Christian Focus Publications, 2004, Page 29
2. Ibid. Page 98
3. Free Church Monthly Record, July-August, 1983
4. Stornoway Gazette Newspaper, April 9, 1983
5. Macritchie, Murdo. :*The Rich Young Ruler*, Audio tape sermon in author's library

CHAPTER ELEVEN: "The Revival of 1984-1986" ('Dusgadh 1984-1986)

1. Maciver, Matthew. *My Portnaguran*, An article retrieved from the internet.
2. Stornoway Gazette Newspaper. October 17, 1995, Page 11
3. Stornoway Gazette Newspaper. October 19, 1995, Page 10
4. Macleod, Donald. Article in the West Highland Free Press, October 27, 1995
5. Macleod, Murdo Alex. Audio tape sermon in author's library

CHAPTER TWELVE: "The Isle of Lewis Today" (Eilean Leodhas An-Diugh)

1. Personal conversation with Alga Hitchcock.
2. Personal conversation with Whitley Garrett, Pastor.
3. Personal conversation with George Ridley.
4. Personal conversation with a couple in the Dumas, Texas church.
5. Personal conversation and correspondence with Sherman Mayfield, Pastor.
6. Personal conversation with Randy Allen, Pastor
7. Macleod, Murdo Alex. A prayer offered in the Free Church, Stornoway. Audio tape in author's library.
8. Macarthur, Allan. Letter written to Steve Taylor by Allan Macarthur on April 3, 2000
9. Peckham, Mary Morrison. *The Lewis Revival*, An article written by Mary Peckham On April 2, 2002
10. Campbell, Duncan. *Tape #5,* Audio tape in author's library
11. Macfarlane, Norman. *Apostles of the North*, The Gazette Office, Stornoway, Page 47
12. Taylor, Steve. *The Skye Revivals*, New Wine Press, 2003, Page 148

13. Peckham, Colin. *The Tide is Out*, An article from Dr. Peckham's website; www. Revivals, org
14. Stornoway Gazette Newspaper, February 26, 2004
15. Campbell, Iain. *Lessons from the Revivals*, An article by Rev. Campbell on www. Backfreechurch.co.uk
16. Searle, David C. *Lewis, Land of Revival, Thirty-five Years After*, Christian Irishman, 1987, Page 2

BIBLIOGRAPHY

BOOKS:

Allen, Brad. *Catch the Wind,* Tarentum, Pennsylvania: Word Association Publishers, 2002

Auld, Alexander. *Ministers and Men in the Far North,* Inverness, Scotland: New Impression, 1956

Beaton, D. *Diary and Sermons of the Rev. Alexander Macleod, Rogart*, Inverness, Scotland, Robert Carruthers and Sons, 1925

Beaton, D. *Some Noted Ministers of the Northern Highlands*, Inverness, Scotland: Northern Counties Newspaper and Printing, 1929

Black, Hugh. *The Clash of Tongues with Glimpses of Revival*, Greenock, Scotland: New Dawn Books, 1988

Blaikie, William. *The Preachers of Scotland*, Edinburgh, Scotland: T. And T. Clark, 1888

Campbell, Murdoch. *Gleanings of Highland Harvest*, Tain, Ross-shire, Scotland: Christian Focus Publications, 1953

Collins, G. N. M. *Big Macrae*, Edinburgh, Scotland: Knox Press, 1976

Ewing, William. *Annals of the Free Church of Scotland: 1843-1900*, Edinburgh, Scotland: T.&T. Clark, 1914

Ferguson, John. *When God Came Down*, Stornoway, Isle of Lewis: Lewis Recordings, 2000

Grant, John. *Disruption Worthies of the Highlands*, Edinburgh, Scotland: 1886

Haswell-Smith, Hamish. *An Island Odyssey*, Edinburgh, Scotland: Canongate Books Ltd., 1999

Jeffrey, Kenneth. *When the Lord Walked the Land*, Carlisle, UK: Paternoster Press, 2002

Kennedy, John. *The Days of the Fathers in Ross-Shire*, Inverness, Scotland: Christian Focus Publications, 1861

Macaulay, Murdo. *Aspects of the Religious History of Lewis*, Inverness, Scotland: John G. Eccles Printers Ltd.,

Macaulay, Murdo. *The Burning Bush of Carloway*, Stornoway, Isle of Lewis: Essprint Ltd., 1984

Macaulay, Murdo. *Free Church Ministers in Lewis: 1843-1993*,

Macdonald, Donald. *Lewis, A History of the Island*, Edinburgh, Scotland: Gordon Wright Publishing, 1978

Macdonald, Kenneth. *Social and Religious Life in the Highlands*, Edinburgh, Scotland: John Smith and Son, 1902

Macfarlane, Norman. *Apostles of the North*, Stornoway, Isle of Lewis: The Gazette Office.

Macfarlane, Norman. *The Men of the Lews*, Stornoway, Isle of Lewis: The Gazette Office, 1924

Macleod, John. *A Brief Record of the Church in Uig*, 1994

Macleod, Norman. *Lewis Revivals of the 20th Century,* Stornoway, Isle of Lewis: Hebridean Press Service, 1988

Macrae, Alexander. *Revivals in the Highlands and Islands*, Hartshill, Stoke-on-Trent: Tentmaker Publications, 1998

Peckham, Colin and Mary. *Sounds from Heaven*, Christian Focus Publications, Fearn, Ross-shire, Scotland, 2004

Roberts, Richard Owen. *Scotland Saw His Glory*, Wheaton, Illinois: International Awakening Press, 1995

Scott, Hew. *Fasti Ecclesiae Scoticanae; The Succession of Ministers in the Church of Scotland from the Reformation*, Edinburgh, Scotland: Oliver and Boyd, 1928

Taylor, Steve. *The Skye Revivals*, Chichester, England: New Wine Press, 2003

West, Morris. *The Summer of the Red Wolf*, New York: William Morrow and Company, Inc., 1971

VIDEO TAPES:

"The Wind of the Spirit", Belfast, Ireland: Ambassador Productions Ltd., 1999

ARTICLES

Campbell, Iain. "Which Revival?". Stornoway Gazette, Stornoway, Isle of Lewis, February 24, 2002

Campbell, Iain. "Lessons from the Revivals". Stornoway Gazette, Stornoway, Isle of Lewis, March 3, 2002

Campbell, Iain. "The Church in Uig". Stornoway Gazette, Isle of Lewis, May 19, 2002

Chalmers, Thomas. "Sermons and Writings", *www.newble.co.uk*

Dumbarton West Kirk. *www.freespace.virin.net*

Free Church Archives. "Fellowship Meetings in the Carloway Revival", *www.freechurch.org*

Free Church Archives. "The Experience of John Macleod (An Cor)", *www.freechurch.org*

Free Church Archives. "An Cor's First Communion", *www.freechurch.org*

Free Church Archives. "The Experience of Old Duncan Macphail", www.freechurch.org

Maciver, Matthew. "My Portnaguran", An article on *www.myportnaguran.blogspot.com*

Memorial Fund Series. "Highland Clearances", *www.tartans.com*

Peckham, Colin. "The Tide is Out", *www.revivals.org*

Peckham, Mary. "The Lewis Revival (1950)" *www.revivals.org*

Scottish Life. Autumn, 2004, Box 403, Vandalia, Ohio

Smith, Kenneth. "Knock Free Church of Scotland"

Stornoway Gazette. "Giving Thanks for 40 Years of Preaching in Uig", Donnie Macinnes, February 26, 2004

Stornoway Gazette. "The Story of a Lewis Catechist", December 25, 1971, January 1, 1972, January 8, 1972, January 15, 1972, January 22, 1972, January 29, 1972, February 5, 1972, February 12, 1972, February 19, 1972, February 26, 1972, March 5, 1972

Stornoway Gazette. October 17, 1995.

Stornoway Gazette, October 19,1995

Taylor, Steve. "The Revival of 1934-39", A letter I received from Steve Taylor, a resident of the Isle of Skye.

United Free Church. "Short History of the United Free Church of Scotland", *www.ufcos.org*

West Highland Free Press. October 27, 1995

AUDIO TAPES:

Campbell, Duncan. "The Lewis Revival", Edinburgh, Scotland: The Faith Mission

Campbell, Duncan. "Principles that Govern Spiritual Awakening", Edinburgh, Scotland: The Faith Mission

Campbell, Duncan. "Conversion Testimony", Audio tape in author's library

Campbell, Duncan. "Revival Tape #4" , Audio tape in author's library

Campbell, Duncan. "Revival Tape #5", Audio tape in author's library

Campbell, Duncan. "When the Fire of God Fell", Audio tape in author's library

Macleod, Murdo Alex. "Go Home and Tell", Audio tape in author's library

Macleod, Murdo Alex and Murdo Macaulay. "Discussion on Revival", Audio tape in author's library

Macritchie, Murdo. "The Rich, Young Ruler", Audio tape in author's library

THE END

(AN DEIREADH)

ABOUT THE AUTHOR

Brad Allen is a Baptist minister from the state of Oklahoma. He served as Pastor of six different churches over a period of forty years. He served as Pastor of the First Baptist Church, Carter, Oklahoma, First Baptist Church, Sentinel, Oklahoma, Central Baptist Church, Lawton, Oklahoma, and finished his pastoral career at the First Baptist Church, Duncan, Oklahoma, serving there for seventeen years.

When he resigned from the pastorate in 1999, Brad Allen began a new career. He is now preaching Spiritual Awakening Conferences across America. In the past four years, He has preached Spiritual Awakening Conferences in thirteen different states, and in Scotland.

Mr. Allen has also fulfilled a long-time dream of writing about revival in the Hebrides Islands. In 2002, his book, *Catch the Wind* was released. It is a story of a great revival on the Isle of Lewis which took place 1949-1953.

Mr. Allen is a graduate of Oklahoma Baptist University, Southwestern Baptist Theological Seminary in Ft. Worth, Texas, and holds a doctorate from the Luther Rice Seminary.

The Land God Chose to Love

For a signed copy, send $18.95
(14.95 + $4.00 s/h) to:

Brad Allen
3210 Timber Ridge Dr
Duncan, Oklahoma 73533
Phone: 580-467-0702
E-mail: bla20@cableone.net
Website: www.bradallen.faithweb.com

www.bn.com
www.borders.com

Order direct from Word Association Publishers
orders@wordassociation.com
1-800-827-7903

12-23-19